THE
CONNECTED THROUGH
CONFLICT
GUIDE

How Couples can Turn Fights into Foundation for Lasting Love

MYRON WINGEN

All rights reserved. No part of this publication may be reproduced, distributed, or transmitted in any form or by any means, including photocopying, recording, or other electronic or mechanical methods, without the prior written permission of the publisher, except in the case of brief quotations embodied in critical reviews and certain other noncommercial uses permitted by copyright law.

Copyright © Myron Wingen, 2024.

Dedication

This book is dedicated to all couples who dare to love deeply and face the inevitable storms of conflict, knowing they hold the potential for tremendous growth and connection.

To the couples who refuse to let fights define them, instead viewing each conflict as an opportunity to understand each other better, establish a stronger foundation, and weave a more durable tapestry of love.

May your road be filled with compassion, courage, and a firm conviction in your love's enduring strength. May your differences serve as bridges to deeper understanding, your vulnerabilities as roads to closer intimacy, and your love as a beacon guiding you through the storms and celebrating the victories of your shared journey.

Acknowledgement

Many people's support and encouragement helped make this book possible.

First and foremost, I'd like to thank the innumerable couples who have boldly shared their stories of love and conflict, hardships and victories, wisdom and resilience. Your experiences have inspired and informed every page of this book.

I am grateful to the therapists, researchers, and authors whose work has highlighted the way to healthy partnerships. Your observations have laid the groundwork for comprehending the complexity of love and conflict.

I'm grateful to my coworkers and friends for providing comments, encouragement, and a listening ear during the writing process. Your assistance has been invaluable.

Finally, I thank my wife for her consistent love, support, and patience during this artistic endeavor. Your presence has consistently inspired and strengthened me.

Why This Book?

A simple yet profound belief inspired this book: while often regarded as the enemy of love, conflict may be its greatest ally. It was designed to help couples perceive conflict as an opportunity to develop their relationship, strengthen their bond, and create a more resilient and rewarding love.

In these pages, you'll find a mix of cutting-edge research, practical tools, and real-life examples to assist you:

- Understand the anatomy of conflict: Learn how disagreements form, why they escalate, and how to effectively resolve them.

- Develop emotional literacy: Learn the language of emotions to express your demands clearly and respond to your partner with empathy.

- Create a safe space for vulnerability: Establish trust and security, allowing both partners to be themselves, even if they disagree.

- Master your communication skills: Learn how to communicate clearly, compassionately, and assertively, particularly in difficult situations.

- Transform conflict into connection: Learn how to utilize arguments to extend your understanding, improve your connections, and develop a stronger relationship.

Whether you're dealing with recurring issues or want to improve your relationship, this book will teach you how to use conflict as a catalyst for more satisfying and meaningful relationships.

Table of Contents

Dedication 2
Acknowledgement 3
Why This Book? 4
Introduction 9

Chapter 1: The Anatomy of a Fight 14
    Decoding the Stages of Conflict 18
    Identifying Your Conflict Triggers 23
    Key Points 25
    Self-Reflection Questions 26

Chapter 2: The Science of Connection and Disconnection 29
    How Our Brains and Bodies React to Conflict 33
    The Role of Attachment in Couple Conflict 36
    Key Points 41
    Self-Reflection Questions 42

Chapter 3: Unveiling Your Conflict Culture 45
    Exploring Your Individual Conflict Styles 49
    Understanding Your Couple Conflict Dance 55
    Key Points 63
    Self-Reflection Questions 64

Chapter 4: The Power of Emotional Awareness 69
    Identifying and Expressing Your Needs 74

Developing Emotional Literacy in Your Relationship..
78
Key Points..83
Self-Reflection Questions... 84

Chapter 5: Mastering the Art of Communication.....88
Active Listening: Hearing Beyond the Words......... 94
Speaking Your Truth with Clarity and Compassion.98
Key Points..103
Self-Reflection Questions... 104

Chapter 6: Creating a Safe Space for Vulnerability.....107
Building Trust and Safety in Your Relationship..... 110
Repairing Ruptures and Rebuilding Connection... 115
Key Points..120
Self-Reflection Questions... 121

Chapter 7: Navigating Common Conflict Scenarios...125
Money Matters: Resolving Financial Disputes......131
Parenting Conflicts: Finding Common Ground..... 136
Key Points..141
Self-Reflection Questions... 142

Chapter 8: The Art of Compromise and Negotiation...146
Moving from Win-Lose to Win-Win Solutions....... 151
Setting Healthy Boundaries and Respecting

Differences...156
Key Points..160
Self-Reflection Questions................................ 161

Chapter 9: Reframing Conflict as an Opportunity. 164
Shifting Perspectives: Seeing the Positive in Disagreements...169
Using Conflict to Deepen Intimacy and Understanding... 173
Key Points..178
Self-Reflection Questions................................ 179

Chapter 10: When Conflict Becomes Unhealthy... 184
Recognizing the Signs of Emotional Abuse..........188
Seeking Help: Therapy and Other Resources...... 191
Key Points..196
Self-Reflection Questions................................ 197

Chapter 11: Cultivating a Culture of Love and Respect..200
Nurturing Appreciation and Gratitude.................. 204
Creating Rituals for Connection and Intimacy...... 207
Key Points..212
Self-Reflection Questions................................ 213

Conclusion... 216
THANK YOU.. 221

Introduction

The air was dense and stifling, crackling with tension. Dinner plates, once full of the promise of a shared meal, now sat abandoned, like fragments of a forgotten discussion. Sarah's shrill, strained voice pierced through the silence. "Mark, it isn't about the dishes! It's about you never seeming to notice or care about my burden around here."

Mark, bent over in his chair and fists clenched, responded, "Here we are again. Why does everything have to be fought over? I work all day, come home weary, and get nothing but criticism." The old dance of accusation and defense had begun, with their words serving as weapons in a conflict they could not win.

Unfortunately, this scene occurs every day in numerous homes. Conflict, in all of its forms, is a common experience in human interactions. Disagreements, whether passionate, seething animosity, or chilly disengagement, are as much a part of our shared human experience as love, laughter, and connection. We disagree on chores, finances, parenting issues, and other seemingly

This book is neither a miracle cure nor a one-size-fits-all approach. Every relationship is unique, and each couple's route to connection will differ. However, the concepts and methods presented here provide a powerful framework for managing the unavoidable obstacles of love and dedication.

As you turn the page, you will begin a journey of self-discovery and relationship development. Prepare to question your conflict assumptions and adopt a new style of interacting with your spouse. Most importantly, prepare to find the tremendous potential of connection on the other side of a conflict. The path can be difficult sometimes, but the benefits - a more profound love, a stronger bond, and a more rewarding relationship - are well worth the effort.

Part 1
<u>Understanding the Landscape of Conflict</u>

Chapter 1: The Anatomy of a Fight

"The most important trip you may take in life is meeting people halfway." – Henry Boyle

This remark says a lot about the delicate dance of compromise that underpins all healthy relationships. It also foreshadows the inherent tension when two people, each with their perspectives and priorities, attempt to travel the same path in life. Couples will undoubtedly endure disagreement in some form or another. Recognizing its basic structure, on the other hand, can assist us in having more constructive discussions.

Consider using a map. A war map, not a geographical location map. This map portrays the typical terrain couples encounter during an argument, highlighting potential hazards and providing route guidance. While each conflict is unique, most follow a predictable pattern, with growing stages that can lead to resolution or a dangerous descent into anarchy.

The first step, known as the "trigger," is typically insignificant. A casual comment, a missed chore, a disagreement over a minor issue - these seemingly negligible sparks can start a big inferno if left unchecked. Recognizing these triggers in ourselves and our partners is essential for preventing escalation. When you criticize your partner, does their tone of voice change? Do you back away when your lover raises their voice? Identifying these little symptoms may allow you to remedy problems before they become more serious.

The conflict enters the "escalation" phase when a trigger is activated. Emotions rise, screams erupt, and accusations fly. This stage is typically distinguished by a back-and-forth exchange of complaints and defenses, with each partner digging in their heels and determined to prove their point. The focus shifts away from the original issue and toward a more significant struggle for power and approval. "You always..." and "You never..." became common refrains, generalizations that fueled frustration.

As the conflict intensifies, our bodies and minds respond. Heart rates increase, muscles tense, and stress hormones surge. We go into "fight-or-flight" mode, prepared to attack or run. As emotions take hold, rational thought loses importance. This physiological response, known as "flooding," may impede our ability to communicate effectively. We become more reactive, less sympathetic, and more likely to say things that we subsequently regret.

If not handled properly, escalation can result in a "standoff." Communication declines, giving place to cold silence or angry comments. Partners can withdraw physically or emotionally, generating estrangement and resentment. The primary issue is lost in the shuffle of hurt feelings and unresolved emotions. This period can linger for hours, days, or weeks, ruining the connection and leaving both couples lonely and misunderstood.

Fortunately, the conflict map also includes paths to "resolution." This needs to shift from attack and defense to comprehension and empathy. It requires a desire to listen, recognize each other's points of view, and find common ground. Resolution may not necessarily imply complete agreement, but it does need a shared commitment to finding a solution that fits both parties' needs.

The path to reconciliation frequently requires "repair attempts"—small acts of compassion that signal a desire to de-escalate and reconcile. A friendly gesture, a humorous comment, or an apology can all help break the ice and start a conversation. Successful couples recognize and respond to these measures to recover their connection, preventing the problem from growing.

The ultimate step in a quarrel is "reconciliation," which comprises reestablishing connection and closeness. This could include expressing regret, requesting forgiveness, or simply confirming your love and devotion. Reconciliation allows you to learn from the conflict, identify patterns that contribute to conflicts, and make intentional choices to improve future communication.

Understanding the anatomy of a conflict is the first step toward transforming it from a destructive force to a catalyst for growth. The journey may be arduous, but the rewards - a stronger connection and a more robust love - are well worth it.

Decoding the Stages of Conflict

Consider the following case: A seemingly regular morning. Sunlight shines through the kitchen window as Alex hums a cheery melody while making breakfast. Still tired from sleep, Chris stumbles into the room with his eyes half-closed. Alex smiles as he greets Chris with a spatula.

Good morning, Sleepyhead! The pancakes are almost ready. Chris grumbles, grabs a coffee mug, and proceeds to the coffee maker. "Ugh, is there no more coffee? "Seriously?" Alex's smile disappears. "Oh, sorry, I haven't had a chance to make a fresh pot yet." Chris smashes the empty carafe onto the countertop. "It's like you don't even consider my needs." The delightful morning takes a surprising turn.

This seemingly insignificant discussion demonstrates the initial step of a conflict: the trigger. Triggers are the initial sparks that start the flame of conflict. They might be subtle (tone of voice, facial expression, forgotten assignment) or overt (critical statement, violated promise, conflict of opinion). Triggers may appear trivial in isolation, but if mishandled, they can snowball into significant disagreements.

Escalation is the second stage, characterized by an increase in emotional intensity. Voices escalate, body language becomes more defensive, and accusations fly. In our hypothetical situation, Alex might respond to Chris' criticism with a defensive retort: "Well, maybe if you got up earlier, you could make your own coffee!" Chris may respond with a harsh remark, transforming the tranquil morning into a heated exchange.

The emphasis frequently transfers from the initial trigger to a more significant power battle during escalation. Past grudges reemerge, and partners may indulge in "kitchen-sinking " or bring up irrelevant things to prove their point. "This isn't just about the coffee; it's about the fact that you never help around the house!" Generalizations like "always" and "never" become weapons, portraying the partner negatively and fanning the flames of conflict.

Our bodies respond as our emotions become more intense. Our heart rate rises, our palms sweat, and our muscles contract. We enter a state of physiological alertness, ready for combat or flight. This "flooding" response may impair our ability to think clearly and speak effectively. We become more reactive, less compassionate, and more prone to saying things we subsequently regret.

The third stage, the standoff, happens after communication fails. Partners can withdraw physically or emotionally, causing estrangement and hatred. The initial issue is submerged in a sea of bitterness and unresolved tension. Alex may hurry out of the kitchen, leaving Chris furious in her wake. Alternatively, they may wage a cold war, exchanging frosty looks and sharp remarks for the day.

Standoffs can last hours, days, or even weeks, poisoning the well of connection and making both partners feel lonely and misunderstood. This stage is critical in the conflict. Will the couple resolve their disagreements and move ahead, or will they remain entrenched in their viewpoints, causing hatred to spread?

The fourth step, resolution, entails transitioning from attack and defense to understanding and empathy. It involves a willingness to listen, comprehend each other's points of view, and discover common ground. Resolution may not always imply perfect agreement, but it does need a mutual commitment to finding a solution that meets both parties' requirements.

In our breakfast situation, resolution may begin with one person stepping back and proposing a repair attempt. "Hey," Chris would begin, "I'm sorry for snapping at you over the coffee." I awoke on the wrong side of my bed. Seeing Chris's attempt to de-escalate, Alex may make a conciliatory gesture. "It's fine, I understand. Mornings are difficult. "How about I make us a new pot and start over?"

The couple could then engage in a more constructive discussion, expressing their needs and concerns without blaming or criticizing. They may acknowledge their role in the conflict, demonstrate a willingness to compromise, and agree to take turns preparing coffee in the morning or clarify their demands in the future.

The final stage, reconciliation, entails reestablishing connections and closeness after the disagreement. This could include expressing regret, seeking forgiveness, or simply confirming your love and backgrounds all influence the development of these sensitive areas.

Identifying your triggers requires introspection and self-awareness. Take some time to consider previous arguments. Observe patterns in your reactions. What sets you off? What statements or actions set you off? Journaling, meditation, and therapy can all aid in self-discovery.

Once you've identified your triggers, consider your partner's. Observe how they respond to arguments. Do they shut down when confronted with powerful emotions? Do they become defensive when asked to help with chores? Pay attention to their nonverbal cues, such as tone of voice, facial expressions, and body language, as they can disclose underlying problems.

Maintaining open communication with your partner is essential. Create a safe environment for discussing your triggers. Share your vulnerabilities with your spouse, and listen with empathy while they share theirs. This shared knowledge fosters compassion and enables you to deal with conflict more sensitively.

Recognizing triggers in the present is crucial for preventing escalation. Seeing your partner's voice rising or their body language tightening suggests a potential trigger activation. Pause, breathe, and reflect on their emotional state. "I see you're upset. "Can we take a break and come back to this later?" This simple act of awareness can alleviate tension and prevent a full-blown dispute.

Identifying and recognizing triggers requires time and compassion for both you and your partner. It's an ongoing journey of self-discovery and relationship building. However, the benefits—a stronger connection, better intimacy, and longer-lasting love—are well worth the effort.

Key Points

- Conflicts often follow a predictable escalation pattern, beginning with a trigger and progressing to a potential standoff, settlement, and reconciliation.

- Recognizing your "conflict triggers" - those sensitive areas that elicit emotional responses - is critical for properly managing disagreements.

- Triggers can come from various sources, including past experiences, personality qualities, and attachment requirements.

- Physiological responses such as "flooding" can impair our ability to communicate appropriately and calmly during conflict.

- Repair attempts, or modest acts of goodwill, can help to de-escalate tensions and open the path for reconciliation.

Self-Reflection Questions

1. Remember a recent argument you had with your partner. What words or actions started the conflict?

_____

_____

_____

_____

_____

2. What bodily sensations do you experience when you are upset about a disagreement? (e.g., a racing heart, tight jaw, and flushed face).

_____

_____

_____

_____

_____

3. What topics or situations cause the most heated argument in your relationship?

_____

_____

_____

_____

_____

4. How do you typically respond when your partner criticizes or expresses disapproval?

_____
_____
_____
_____
_____

5. What tendencies does your partner have that remind you of your insecurities or past hurts?

_____
_____
_____
_____
_____

Chapter 2: The Science of Connection and Disconnection

"The best and most beautiful things in the world cannot be seen or even touched - they must be felt with the heart." -
Helen Keller

Keller's words emphasize the enormous strength of human connection, a force that transcends the physical realm and penetrates the very core of our being. At their best, personal relationships provide a solid foundation upon which we can venture into the world, knowing we have a haven to return to. However, these same links can bring significant distress and isolation, particularly during conflict.

Understanding the physics of connection and detachment can explain why arguments unfold. Our thoughts and bodies, well-tuned for survival, react to perceived threats with a sequence of physiological responses. Consider an early human encountering a saber-toothed tiger. Their hearts race, their respiration quickens, and their muscles tighten as they prepare to fight or flee. This "fight-or-flight" response, which is required for survival in dangerous situations, can override our rational mind during interpersonal conflict.

When a fight with our spouse elicits this essential response, we enter a state called "flooding." Blood pressure rises, stress hormones increase and cognitive abilities diminish. We lose our ability to think logically, empathically, and communicate effectively. Instead, we act rashly, driven by fear, hatred, or a frantic need to protect ourselves.

This flood response explains why, during arguments, we may say or do things we subsequently regret. Our words become weapons, our tone becomes harsh, and our body language shows aggression or withdrawal. We may interrupt, criticize, or make broad generalizations, igniting conflict.

The Gottman Method identifies four unique behaviors that suggest flooding and predict relationship distress: criticism, contempt, defensiveness, and stonewalling. Criticism involves attacking your partner's character rather than addressing a specific behavior. Contempt, the most destructive of the four, expresses scorn or disrespect through sarcasm, mockery, or angry humor. Defensiveness involves shifting responsibility and avoiding accountability. Stonewalling manifests as retreat, breakdown in communication, and refusal to participate.

These "Four Horsemen of the Apocalypse," as the Gottmans call them, wreak havoc on relationships by weakening trust, intimacy, and connection. Recognizing these tendencies in ourselves and our partners is essential for breaking bad habits and creating a more positive dynamic.

However, the study of relationships extends beyond detachment and emphasizes the vast powers that unite us. Attachment theory, a fundamental idea in relationship science, explains how our early childhood experiences influence our lifelong patterns of connection. These patterns, called attachment types, influence how we seek comfort, stability, and connection in adult relationships.

Individuals with a stable attachment style are frequently satisfied with intimacy and liberty. They approach relationships with trust and confidence, seeking help and soothing their partners during difficult times. Those with an anxious attachment type are always seeking connection and are terrified of being abandoned. They may become too involved with their relationship, requiring frequent reassurance and reinforcement. Avoidant attachment patterns prioritize independence while suppressing feelings. They may struggle with intimacy and withdraw amid disagreements.

Understanding your and your partner's attachment styles may provide valuable insights into your conflict patterns. An anxiously attached person, for example, may be easily triggered by perceived distance or a partner's lack of response. When emotionally charged, an avoidantly attached individual may withdraw or shut down.

The science of relationships offers a compelling lens through which to evaluate human interactions. Understanding the neurological and psychological mechanisms at work helps us become more aware of our and our partner's emotions. This knowledge allows us to negotiate disputes with greater competence, compassion, and intention, transforming them into chances for deeper understanding and more resilient love.

How Our Brains and Bodies React to Conflict

Consider this: you're walking alone at night when something strange emerges from an alleyway. Your blood pressure rises quickly, muscles tighten, and your senses sharpen. This built-in reaction, known as the "fight-or-flight" response, is your body's way of preparing you to face danger or flee for safety. It's a primitive mechanism built into our neurological system to safeguard us from harm.

Assume this situation: you are in a heated conflict with your partner. Accusations fly, voices are raised, and emotions flare. While there is no physical threat, your body reacts in a very equivalent manner. Your heart was beating, your palms were sweating, and your cheeks were flushed. Your brain system perceives the emotional intensity of the dispute as a physical threat, eliciting the same fight-or-flight response.

This physiological reaction, sometimes known as "flooding," can significantly obstruct effective communication during conflict. Our reasoning mind gives way to our primal instincts when confronted with overwhelming circumstances. We lose empathy, rationality, and subtle communication abilities. Instead, we react instantly, motivated by fear, hatred, or a desperate need to protect ourselves.

Flood-related physiological changes may manifest in several ways. Your heart beats, your breathing quickens, and your muscles contract. You may experience intestinal discomfort, dizziness, or nausea. Your voice may tremble, your hands quiver, and your cheeks flush or pale. These biological sensations can intensify emotions, creating a vicious cycle of reactions.

Flooding impacts the prefrontal cortex, which is responsible for rational thought, decision-making, and emotional regulation. This explains why, during arguments, we could say or do things we later regret. Our words become weapons, our tone becomes harsh, and our body language displays rage or defensiveness. We may interrupt, criticize, or make broad generalizations, fanning the flames of dispute.

Flooding also reduces our ability to analyze data efficiently. We may misinterpret our partner's words or behavior and assume aggressive intent when none exists. We may selectively focus on material that reinforces our negative beliefs while rejecting evidence to the contrary. This distorted view can lead to misunderstandings, escalate conflict, and increase the gap between partners.

The Gottman Method identifies particular behaviors that typically accompany flooding and indicate relationship difficulties. Criticism, disdain, defensiveness, and stonewalling are only a few examples. Criticism is about undermining your partner's character rather than addressing specific behavior. Contempt is the most harmful, showing scorn or disrespect through sarcasm, mockery, or angry humor. Defensiveness involves shifting responsibility and avoiding accountability. Stonewalling manifests as retreat, cutting off communication, and refusing to participate.

Recognizing these behaviors in ourselves and our partners is crucial to ending destructive cycles and creating a more positive dynamic. We can take steps to de-escalate the situation when we notice signs of flooding, whether in our bodies or in our partner's actions. This could entail taking a break from the conversation, practicing relaxation techniques, or simply acknowledging the emotional intensity of the issue.

The Role of Attachment in Couple Conflict

Envision a toddler slipping and scraping their knees. They scream out, yearning for solace from their caregiver. The caregiver's response - a soothing hug, a reassuring remark, or a dismissive glare - influences the child's developing knowledge of relationships and their place in the world. This early dance of connection and dissociation creates the groundwork for our attachment styles or habits of relating that we take into adult relationships.

Attachment theory, an essential component of relationship science, posits that our early attachments to caregivers impact our expectations and behaviors in intimate relationships. These relationships influence how we seek intimacy, deal with conflict, and manage our emotions. Although attachment styles are not fixed, they are typically consistent throughout life. We can change these behaviors and make more secure connections by becoming more aware of ourselves and making intentional efforts.

Researchers have identified four basic attachment styles: secure, anxious, avoidant, and fearful-avoidant (disorganized). Securely attached individuals received consistent and responsive care during their formative years. They believe they deserve love and will be supported by others. They handle relationships with impressive convenience, taking on both intimacy and independence.

Anxiously attached people, on the other hand, may have received inconsistent or unintended caregiving. They frequently worry about their partner's availability and response and seek reassurance and confirmation. They may become concerned with the relationship, fearing abandonment and engaging in clinging behavior.

Avoidantly attached people frequently had caretakers who were emotionally aloof or contemptuous. They learned to control their emotions and rely on their resources. They may appear independent and self-sufficient, yet they frequently struggle with intimacy and vulnerability. During conflict, they may withdraw or detach themselves for fear of being engulfed or emotionally overwhelmed.

The toughest of the four kinds of attachment is fearful-avoidant attachment, which is caused by trauma or abuse. Individuals with this type demonstrate a combination of nervous and avoidant tendencies. They want connection yet avoid intimacy, frequently engaged in push-and-pull dynamics. They may struggle with trust and engage in unpredictable conduct.

These attachment patterns profoundly impact how partners feel and manage conflict. Securely bonded individuals approach arguments calmly and confidently. They communicate their demands clearly, actively listen to their partner's point of view, and work together to discover solutions. They recover swiftly from confrontation, retaining a sense of trust and connection even when disagreeing.

Anxiously connected people may perceive conflict as threatening their relationship, worrying that disputes may result in abandonment. They may become overly sensitive to their partner's cues, seeing any perceived distance or criticism as a sign of rejection. They may exhibit protest behaviors such as excessive reassurance-seeking or clinging, which can unintentionally drive their spouse away.

Avoidantly attached individuals frequently perceive disagreement as an incursion into their autonomy. They may withdraw or shut down emotionally to retain control and prevent vulnerability. They may prioritize independence over closeness, resulting in low emotional engagement and trouble resolving disagreements productively.

During the confrontation, fearful-avoidant people may exhibit unpredictable actions, alternating between wanting to be close to their spouse and pulling away. They may struggle with trust and have high emotional reactivity. They may misread their partner's actions, resulting in miscommunication and aggression.

Understanding your attachment style and spouse's can provide crucial insights into your conflict patterns. It enables you to identify the underlying demands and concerns that shape your reactions.

This knowledge can increase compassion for yourself and your spouse, paving the path for more effective communication and conflict resolution.

For example, if you understand how your partner's anxious attachment style relates to their increased sensitivity during conflicts, you can respond with more understanding and comfort. If you recognize your avoidant tendencies, you can deliberately remain present and engaged during a disagreement, even if it is uncomfortable.

Working with a therapist can provide a safe environment for investigating attachment patterns and building more secure attachments. Couples therapy can help partners better understand one another's needs, communicate more effectively, and establish a stronger foundation of trust and connection.

Attachment theory provides a robust framework for analyzing the processes of attachment and separation in partnerships. Recognizing the impact of our attachment styles allows us to acquire self-awareness, develop compassion for our relationships, and change disagreement from a source of grief to an opportunity for growth and deeper connection.

Key Points

- Our minds and bodies have an integrated alarm mechanism (fight-or-flight reaction) that kicks in when we detect a threat, such as interpersonal conflict.

- "Flooding," or physiological overwhelm, can impair our ability to think clearly, talk effectively, and empathize with our partners during disagreements.

- The Gottman Method identifies four communication patterns (criticism, contempt, defensiveness, and stonewalling) that signal distress and predict relationship breakdown.

- Attachment theory explains how early childhood experiences shape our relating patterns and adult behavior.

- Understanding your attachment style and that of your partner will help you get insight into your conflict patterns and handle conflicts more productively.

Self-Reflection Questions

1. Think back to a recent dispute with your partner. Did you notice an indication of flooding in yourself or your partner? (e.g., racing heart, difficulty listening, defensive responses)

_____
_____
_____
_____
_____

2. Which of the "Four Horsemen" (criticism, contempt, defensiveness, and stonewalling) do you use frequently during conflict?

_____

_____

_____

_____

_____

3. How would you describe your early childhood interactions with primary caregivers? Did consistency, warmth, and responsiveness define it, or was it more unexpected and distant?

_____

_____

_____

_____

_____

4. Which attachment style (secure, anxious, avoidant, or fearful-avoidant) best describes your experiences in intimate relationships?

_____

_____

_____

_____

_____

5. How might your and your spouse's attachment styles influence your conflict patterns?

_____

_____

_____

_____

_____

Chapter 3: Unveiling Your Conflict Culture

"We are all shaped by the forces that have acted upon us." -
Robert Greene

Greene's remarks resonate strongly in relationships, where our past experiences, inherited behavior, and cultural influences combine to produce a distinct "conflict culture." This culture, which is frequently unseen but profoundly established, influences how we handle arguments, express emotions, and seek solutions. Understanding your conflict culture and your partner's is like understanding a secret language that is essential to unlocking deeper connections and handling arguments more easily.

Think of a family dining table. Voices rise, fights flare, and emotions overflow like a pot boiling over. This scene witnessed throughout childhood, may instill a sense that disagreement is explosive and harmful. Perhaps you grew up in a household where arguments were unacknowledged, boiling below the surface like a secret volcano. These early experiences impact our perception of conflict and how it should be handled.

Our families of origin act as training grounds for our conflict culture. We see how our parents and siblings deal with disagreements, absorbing their communication methods, coping mechanisms, and conflict-resolution strategies. If your parents handled conflict via open conversation and compromise, you might approach disputes in the same collaborative spirit. If they avoided conflict at all costs, you may follow suit, ignoring your needs or retiring at the first indication of friction.

Cultural norms play an essential part in establishing our conflict culture. Some cultures favor conflict and intense expression, while others value tranquility and indirect communication. These cultural scripts shape how we interpret conflict, express our emotions, and seek solutions. Couples from different cultural origins may need help with difficulties since their expectations and communication techniques differ, resulting in misunderstandings and frustrations.

Beyond family and society, our personalities and attachment types contribute to our distinct conflict culture. Introverts prefer to absorb their feelings inside before arguing, whereas extroverts may benefit from open and rapid communication. Anxiously attached individuals may seek reassurance and intimacy during a quarrel, whereas avoidantly attached individuals may prioritize independence and emotional distance.

Recognizing these many variables might help you better understand your conflict responses and your partner's. It enables you to transcend preconceptions and assumptions, replacing them with curiosity and compassion. Instead of categorizing your spouse as "difficult" or "unreasonable," consider their behaviors through the prism of their specific conflict culture.

The Gottman Method distinguishes three conflict styles: validators, avoiders, and volatiles. Validators prioritize comprehension and compromise. They express their emotions calmly, listen carefully to their partner's point of view, and work together to discover mutually acceptable solutions. Avoiders prefer to minimize conflict by repressing their emotions or withdrawing from arguments.

They may prioritize maintaining unity over resolving fundamental difficulties. Volatiles engage in intense and expressive disputes, which are generally marked by loud voices, dramatic gestures, and strong beliefs. They thrive on debate and see disagreement as an opportunity for connection and intimacy.

While each style has strengths and challenges, no style is intrinsically "better" than the others. The key is understanding how your style interacts with your partner's. For example, a validator coupled with an avoider may have difficulty addressing their needs because the avoider's tendency to withdraw can leave the validator feeling unheard. Two volatile individuals may be in a perpetual power struggle, with intense exchanges culminating in explosive conflicts.

Recognizing your couple's "conflict dance" - the interplay of your styles - can provide valuable insights into your interaction patterns. It lets you foresee prospective obstacles and design more effective conflict-resolution techniques. A validator and avoider, for example, may benefit from setting explicit communication standards that ensure both partners feel comfortable expressing their wants and concerns. Two volatile individuals may agree on a "time-out" signal to prevent escalation and allow for emotional regulation.

Understanding your conflict culture is about recognizing the forces that have molded your conflict responses and learning how to handle conflicts in a way that respects your and your partner's needs. This journey of self-discovery and mutual understanding can result in a more peaceful and meaningful relationship in which conflict, rather than dividing you, catalyzes deeper connection and a more robust love.

Exploring Your Individual Conflict Styles

Think about a dance floor. Couples sway to the music, each dancing with their rhythm and elegance. Some people move effortlessly across the floor, their steps synced and harmonious. Others dance with enthusiasm, their bodies entangled in a maelstrom of intensity. Some couples cautiously handle the space, keeping a comfortable distance and avoiding collisions. Like conflict types in relationships, these dance styles reflect personal preferences, temperaments, and taught habits.

Individuals approach conflict uniquely, just as no two dances are the same. Some people approach arguments head-on, eager to share their thoughts and work things out. Others choose to avoid confrontation to maintain harmony and minimize emotional intensity. Some people find themselves locked in a push-and-pull cycle, alternating between engagement and disengagement.

Understanding your personal conflict style is similar to discovering your distinct dance steps. It enables you to predict your natural impulses, foresee potential traps, and devise effective conflict resolution solutions. It also allows for deeper understanding and compassion for your partner, whose conflict style may differ significantly from yours.

The Gottman Method, a research-based approach to relationship health, distinguishes three main conflict styles: validators, avoiders, and volatiles. Each style has its qualities, strengths, and challenges.

As the name implies, validators value understanding and mutual regard. They approach disputes with a cool and measured temperament, attempting to understand their partner's point of view before expressing their own. They value compromise and teamwork, seeking win-win solutions that benefit both parties. Validators are excellent at active listening, exhibiting empathy, and identifying common ground. Even when they disagree, they tend to communicate calmly and measuredly.

In contrast, avoiders prefer to avoid conflict. They may control their emotions, shift the subject, or withdraw from heated talks. While their peacemaking intentions are typically reasonable, their avoidance methods might result in unsolved difficulties and simmering hatred. Avoiders may struggle to express their demands directly, thinking that doing so may shatter peace or result in rejection.

Volatiles thrive on intense, outspoken interactions. They approach conflict with zeal and excitement, daring to express themselves and engage in vibrant debate. They appreciate honesty and sincerity, even if it means raising their voices or expressing intense emotions. While their intensity is exciting, it can lead to escalation and wounded feelings if not appropriately managed.

To help you discover your dominant conflict style, examine the following self-assessment questions:

1. When a disagreement occurs, do you usually:

    A. Try to grasp your partner's point of view before expressing your own?

    B. Try to avoid or minimize the conflict?

    C. Participate in a lively debate, expressing your views with passion and conviction?

2. Do you usually do the following during a heated argument?

    A. Remain calm and determined to find a solution.

    B. End or depart from the conversation?

C. Express your feelings assertively, even if it means raising your voice.

3. When it comes to settling disagreements, do you prioritize?

A. Finding a compromise that works for both you and your partner?

B. Maintaining peace and harmony, even ignoring your desires?

C. Ensuring that your voice is heard and your thoughts are respected?

4. How comfortable are you expressing rage or irritation in your relationship?

A. I express myself quietly and constructively.

B. I try to avoid expressing anger or irritation immediately.

C. I express myself openly and passionately.

5. How do you generally handle criticism from your partner?

    A. I actively listen and strive to comprehend their point of view.

    B. I react defensively or retreat from the discourse.

    C. I make a strong counter-critique or argument.

If your answers tend to be "A," you most likely follow the validator style. If "B" resonates more intensely, you may be an avoider. If "C" describes your typical responses, you may recognize yourself as volatile.

Remember that these styles are not fixed groupings. Most people use a variety of styles based on the situation, their mood, and the interplay of their connection. The idea is not to label yourself or your partner but to increase self-awareness and better understand your unique approaches to conflict.

This understanding can help you negotiate arguments more successfully. Validators, for example, may benefit from being more aggressive, ensuring a desire for compromise does not eclipse their requirements. Avoiders might practice expressing their emotions more directly to keep resentment at bay. Volatiles may also consider moderating their emotional intensity, ensuring their enthusiasm does not turn into hostility or overwhelm their spouse.

Understanding Your Couple Conflict Dance

Look at a couple's conflict style as a dancing move influenced by their unique experiences and personalities. When these two distinct patterns combine on the dance floor of a relationship, they form a "conflict dance," a pattern of interaction that can either flow smoothly or result in a step collision. Recognizing each partner's preferred actions is critical for managing disputes gently and turning potential conflicts into chances for connection.

Let us go over the three main conflict styles: validators, avoiders, and volatiles. Each style provides a unique flavor to the dance floor. Validators, or peacemakers, prioritize mutual understanding and compromise. They approach arguments calmly and collectively, attentively listening to their partner's point of view and seeking solutions that benefit both parties. Diplomats are conflict-avoiders who often deny their wants to maintain harmony. Volatiles, or passionate performers, express themselves with flaming intensity, seeing disagreement as a vital, if occasionally explosive, form of connection.

When two validators collaborate, their dispute dance frequently resembles a lovely waltz, marked by mutual respect and a cooperative spirit. They effortlessly acknowledge each other's feelings, negotiate limits with elegance, and thrive at finding mutually beneficial solutions. Disagreements rarely become destructive because they can de-escalate tension and find common ground. For example, if one partner expresses dissatisfaction with a domestic chore imbalance, the other may answer, "I hear you. I understand how it feels unfair. Let's figure out how to distribute the tasks more equitably."

However, even this happy pairing has inherent hazards. The desire to keep the peace might lead to avoidance of essential conversations, enabling bitterness to grow beneath the surface. Both spouses may prefer harmony over expressing their genuine needs, resulting in a buildup of unspoken feelings. Consider a partnership in which both parties consistently agree on their partner's restaurant choices but secretly desire something else. Over time, this might result in feelings of invisibility and contempt. To maintain a good balance, validator couples must prioritize honest communication, ensuring both partners feel comfortable voicing problems and exerting wants.

When an avoider and a validator partner up, their dance becomes a delicate tango that demands cautious navigation and a deep awareness of each other's steps. The validator's desire for open communication and emotional expression may conflict with the avoider's natural tendency to withdraw or suppress feelings. The validator may feel unheard and unappreciated, while the avoider may feel pressed and overwhelmed by their partner's feelings. For example, if the validator initiates a conversation about a recurring issue, the avoider may respond silently or humorously, leaving the validator feeling ignored and dissatisfied.

This combination flourishes when both partners make a concerted effort to bridge the gap between their styles. The validator can demonstrate tolerance and empathy by acknowledging their partner's need for space and time to process feelings. Instead of demanding a speedy conclusion, they should say, "I understand this is a difficult subject for you. Can we take a break and come back to it when you are ready? The avoider, in turn, can practice expressing needs clearly and engaging in open communication, even if it is difficult.

They should practice utilizing "I" phrases to communicate their sentiments without criticizing their partner, such as "I feel overwhelmed when we have these late-night conversations." Can we discuss this in the morning instead?

The dance between two avoiders frequently resembles a slow, careful foxtrot marked by a shared aversion to confrontation. They may prioritize preserving a false impression of calm, brushing difficulties under the rug, or agreeing to disagree. While this technique reduces overt conflict, it can result in resentment and unresolved challenges, similar to a tune with a missing beat. Consider a couple who frequently avoids discussing their financial problems, resulting in increased worry and distrust about money matters.

For this pairing to succeed, both parties must improve their conflict resolution skills and accept that constructive disagreement can deepen the relationship. They can learn to assert their wants, listen actively, and reach mutually beneficial agreements. It takes effort and practice to master a new dance step, but the result is a more rewarding and genuine connection.

When a volatile and a validator dance together, their connection can be like a dynamic salsa, full of passion and diplomacy. The volatile's fiery energy and expressiveness can elicit excitement and promote growth. In contrast, the validator's relaxed attitude and emphasis on compromise can moderate the volatile's intensity and prevent escalation. For example, the volatile may show dissatisfaction with a burst of energy, whereas the validator replies calmly and concentrates on finding a solution.

However, this coupling brings its own set of issues. The volatile's penchant for making big presentations and expressing solid opinions can overwhelm the validator, who may feel forced to yield or deny their needs. The validator's need for calm debate may conflict with the volatile's need for passionate expression, resulting in irritation and misunderstandings. Consider the volatile spouse expressing fury over a missed deadline while the validator tries to calm them down without addressing the underlying issue. This can leave the volatile feeling invalidated while the validator feels useless.

To overcome these hurdles, volatile people might practice expressing their emotions with greater sensitivity and restraint, such as pausing before replying and carefully selecting words. The validator can learn to establish their demands and boundaries more strongly, such as saying, "I understand you're upset, but please speak to me respectfully." Both couples can benefit from improving their active listening and compromise skills, ensuring their voices are heard and appreciated.

The dance between two volatiles can be passionate flamenco, with furious exchanges, dramatic flourishes, and raw emotions. They thrive on debate and see disagreement as an opportunity for connection and intimacy. While typically loud and emotional, their arguments rarely result in long-term bitterness. They have a rare ability to reconcile as fiercely as they quarrel, reinforcing their love and dedication. This could be an intense debate over a political subject, followed by a passionate reconciliation that deepens their friendship.

However, if unchecked, this fiery interplay can be catastrophic. Escalation can spiral out of hand, resulting in cruel words and broken emotions. Consider a debate about a parenting decision that turns into personal assaults and name-calling. To maintain a healthy balance, volatile couples must learn to control their emotions, exercise active listening, and devise conflict resolution solutions before they escalate. Like experienced dancers, they must learn to anticipate each other's movements and adapt their rhythms to avoid collisions.

The most challenging dance is often performed between a volatile and an avoider. The volatile's impassioned expressiveness and desire for engagement contrast with the avoider's propensity to withdraw and avoid conflict. The volatile may feel annoyed and ignored, whereas the avoider may feel swamped and pressed. Like mismatched dancing partners, this pairing necessitates patience, understanding, and compromise to achieve a rhythm that works for everyone. For example, suppose the volatile confronts their spouse about a perceived lack of affection. In that case, the avoider may respond by shutting down or leaving the room, making the volatile feel abandoned and rejected.

Volatile people might learn to approach conflict with greater empathy, acknowledging their partner's need for space and time to process emotions. They can say, "I can tell how you're talking; you're stressed out right now. Can we take a break and return to it later? The avoider, in turn, can practice expressing their demands clearly and engaging in open conversation, even if it is difficult.

They could try saying, "I need some time to think about this before we continue the conversation." Both partners can benefit from learning active listening and compromise skills, which will help them create a place where both views are heard and respected. Adapting to each other's styles is essential for achieving harmony in their dance.

Understanding your couple's conflict dance is equivalent to understanding the precise steps of a complex choreography. It calls for self-awareness, honest communication, and a readiness to adapt and evolve together.

Key Points

A. Your "conflict culture" is a distinct pattern influenced by your upbringing, personality, and cultural background. It determines how you approach obstacles and express yourself during conflict.

B. There are three basic conflict styles:

- Validators (who stress understanding and compromise).
- Avoiders (who prefer to minimize conflict).
- Volatiles (who engage in passionate and expressive disagreement).

C. No one conflict style is fundamentally "better" than another. The idea is to understand how your style interacts with your partner's.

D. Different combinations of conflict types present unique problems and opportunities in relationships.

E. Recognizing your "couple conflict dance" - the interaction of your distinct styles - can help you foresee prospective obstacles and negotiate arguments more productively.

Self-Reflection Questions

1. Consider a typical conflict with your partner. How do you usually handle these situations? Do

you express your emotions honestly, avoid conflict, or engage in heated debate?

_____
_____
_____
_____

2. Think of your family's background. How did your parents and siblings resolve conflicts? Did they express their emotions freely, avoid disagreements, or participate in passionate debate?

_____
_____
_____
_____

3. Consider your cultural background. Is confrontation valued in your society, or is indirect communication preferred? How might this affect your approach to conflict?

_____
_____
_____
_____
_____

4. What are your conflict-resolution strengths and weaknesses? Are you adept at listening, negotiating, or assertively expressing your needs?

_____
_____
_____
_____
_____

5. How does your partner tend to handle conflict? Do they share your style, or do they take a different approach? How might this distinction present obstacles or possibilities in your relationship?

_____
_____

Part 2
Building a Foundation for Healthy Conflict

Chapter 4: The Power of Emotional Awareness

"Unexpressed emotions will never die. They are buried alive and will come forth later in uglier ways." - Sigmund Freud

Freud's ideas highlight a fundamental truth: emotions require awareness. When we hide or ignore our feelings, they don't just go away; they fester and resurface, often in twisted and deadly ways. Emotional awareness, or the ability to observe, understand, and effectively convey our emotions, is critical for positive relationships and dispute resolution.

Visualize a volcano. Molten lava churns under its ostensibly dormant surface, accumulating pressure until it erupts. Similarly, unexpressed emotions accumulate, generating internal stress that might manifest as rage, withdrawal, or sudden outbursts. Emotional awareness acts as a release valve, allowing us to manage our emotions before they become critical.

The journey to self-discovery begins with cultivating an attentive inner presence. Throughout the day, take breaks to focus on yourself. Pay attention to the sensations in your own body. Do you have a tightness in your chest, an aching in your stomach, or a clenched jaw? These physical manifestations reveal essential information about your emotional state. Perhaps you experience a surge of anxiety when presented with an upcoming deadline or a flood of melancholy when you recall a painful experience.

Expressing these emotions and accepting their presence without judgment is the first step toward understanding their significance. Instead of suppressing or ignoring your feelings, allow yourself to fully experience them, viewing them as messengers conveying crucial information about your inner reality.

Consider anger, which is generally seen negatively. While wrath can be destructive, it also serves a valuable purpose. It acts as a signal, alerting us to perceived injustices, unmet requests, or boundary violations. When we ignore or suppress our anger, we miss out on the opportunity to address the root causes of the problem.

The anger may escalate when your partner constantly dismisses your concerns about domestic responsibilities. This wrath may mask a more fundamental yearning for respect, fairness, or a sense of shared responsibility. Recognizing and investigating the source of your anger gives you valuable insight into your needs and motivations. You may find that the chore imbalance leads to sentiments of being underappreciated or taken for granted.

Similarly, melancholy, often regarded as a weakness, delivers essential messages. It could represent a loss, a need for connection, or a separation from your inner self. When you fully accept your sadness, you create space for healing and progress. Perhaps you are devastated when your sweetheart cancels date night for the third time. This grieving may signal a need for quality time and a deeper relationship.

Fear, another emotion sometimes associated with guilt, is a protective mechanism, alerting us to potential threats or vulnerabilities. Perhaps you are terrified when your partner raises their voice, which triggers memories of previous arguments or childhood events. By expressing your fear, you can begin to address its underlying causes and develop appropriate coping strategies. You may note that the loud voice instills a dread of abandonment or a sense of powerlessness.

Developing emotional literacy, or the ability to notice, understand, and express emotions effectively, requires practice and a willingness to broaden your emotional vocabulary. Expand your vocabulary beyond basic terms like "happy" and "sad." Discover the nuances of feelings like satisfaction, joy, gratitude, disappointment, sadness, and impatience. The more nuanced your emotional language, the more accurately you can explain your inner experiences.

Pay attention to the physical feelings that accompany each emotion. Is nervousness represented by a racing heart or shallow breathing? Does sadness feel like a weight on your chest or a loss of energy? Connecting physical experiences to emotional labels broadens your understanding and helps you recognize emotions in yourself and others.

Expressing emotions constructively is another crucial aspect of emotional literacy. This means expressing your feelings honestly and softly without criticizing or abusing your spouse. "I" statements may be helpful. Instead of saying, "You always make me angry," try saying, "I get angry when I feel unheard during our disagreements." This change in vocabulary highlights your personal experiences rather than assigning blame.

Understanding your feelings is just one facet of emotional awareness; you must also know your partner's emotional state. Pay attention to verbal and nonverbal cues. Do their words match their tone of voice and body language? Are they joyful, sad, or frustrated? Empathy is the ability to put oneself in your partner's shoes and understand their perspective.

When your partner expresses emotion, acknowledge and validate their sentiments. "I hear you're hurt. Tell me more about what is happening. This validation promotes a sense of safety and open communication. It indicates to your partner that you care about their feelings and will listen without judgment.

Remember that emotions are not good or bad; they are signals that reveal information about our inner reality.

Identifying and Expressing Your Needs

Visualize a garden. Every plant grows in a specific habitat and requires particular levels of nutrients, water, and sunlight. Similarly, in a relationship, each partner has specific emotional requirements that must be addressed to thrive. Identifying and articulating these needs creates the foundation for a healthy and fulfilling relationship.

Think about your emotional needs as your compass pointing you toward a more contented life. From basic requirements for safety and security to more deep yearnings for connection, intimacy, and belonging, these needs cover a broad spectrum. Unmet needs can produce emotional suffering, leading to conflict, resentment, and estrangement.

One way to determine your emotional requirements is to think about occasions when you were pleased and fulfilled in your relationship. What variables contributed to the pleasant experiences? Perhaps your lover surprised you with a beautiful gesture, making you feel truly loved and treasured. Sometimes, you experience a sense of security and stability when they offer support during a difficult moment. These periods supply crucial signals regarding your underlying emotional requirements.

Consider occasions when you felt hurt, frustrated, or distant from your relationship. What specific incidents lead to such terrible feelings? Perhaps you felt neglected since your partner regularly stressed work over quality time with you. Maybe you felt disrespected when they ignored your opinions during a debate. These encounters may show unmet aspirations for connection, respect, or autonomy.

Another excellent exercise is reviewing a list of everyday emotional demands and assessing which resonates most with you. Some typical needs consist of:

- Security: Feeling safe, stable, and protected in a relationship.

- Connection: A feeling of closeness, intimacy, and belonging with your spouse.
- Autonomy is the ability to express yourself and make your own decisions.
- Meaning: Feeling a feeling of purpose and shared values in your connection.
- Growth: Having the opportunity to study, advance, and widen your horizons together.

Once you've determined your critical emotional requirements, the following stage is to convey them effectively to your partner. This necessitates vulnerability, honesty, and a desire to express oneself genuinely. Choose a time when you both are calm and ready to talk openly and honestly.

Use "I" expressions to explain your requirements without blaming or criticizing your spouse. For example, instead of declaring, "You never make me feel loved," say, "I need to feel more affection and appreciation in our relationship." This strategy focuses on your personal experience and enables your partner to comprehend your point of view.

Be explicit about your expectations and provide practical examples. Instead of expressing, "I need more quality time," try this: "I would love it if we could have a date night once a week where we can focus solely on each other." This clarity enables your partner to grasp your expectations and conduct actual efforts to meet your requirements.

Remember that expressing your wishes does not imply that your partner must change; instead, it asks them to contribute to establishing a more rewarding relationship for both of you. Approach the matter constructively, striving to understand each other's requirements and build mutually beneficial solutions.

This strategy relies significantly on active listening. Listen carefully without interrupting or appearing defensive when your partner mentions a need. Reflect on what you've heard to ensure you get their viewpoint. This expresses respect and indicates that you regard their feelings.

Negotiation and compromise are also crucial to achieving each other's requirements. Recognize that not every desire can be satisfied promptly or completely. Be open to innovative ideas and make sacrifices where necessary. This collaborative approach develops teamwork and deepens friendship.

Identifying and expressing your emotional needs is an ongoing process, not a single event. Expectations may vary as you mature and adjust. Regularly check in with yourself and your spouse, establishing a comfortable setting for open conversation and mutual support.

Developing Emotional Literacy in Your Relationship

Think of emotions as a language—a sophisticated system of signals and indications that expresses our inner experience. Emotional literacy is fluency in this language—that is, the capacity to recognize your own emotions and interpret those of your partner reasonably. This fluency is crucial for navigating every relationship's inevitable ups and downs.

Picture a couple arguing about finances. While one spouse is annoyed by what they believe to be their partner's lack of trust in their capacity to handle money, another is nervous about unanticipated spending. This conflict could spiral into accusations and defensiveness without emotional literacy. But with emotional literacy, each partner may express their underlying emotions—"I feel anxious and overwhelmed," or "I feel frustrated and unappreciated," for example—enabling more effective and sympathetic communication.

Expanding your emotional vocabulary first helps you develop emotional literacy. Though our language is simple—that of "happy," "sad," or "angry," the reality of human experience is significantly more complex. Discover the whole range of feelings: contentment, enthusiasm, thanksgiving, disappointment, grief, guilt, and many more. The richer your emotional vocabulary, the more precisely you can convey your inner world.

Think of it like learning a new language. Initially, you may know a few basic phrases. But as you develop your vocabulary, you can express yourself more eloquently and understand more complex conversations. Similarly, by increasing your emotional vocabulary, you obtain a deeper grasp of your inner landscape and communicate more effectively with your partner.

Next, connect these emotional labels to the bodily feelings they produce. Does anxiety express itself as a racing heart or a knot in your stomach? Does sadness feel heavy in your chest or drain your energy? By associating physical experiences with emotional labels, you increase your understanding and detect emotions more quickly in yourself and others.

Imagine a friend telling you they're "stressed." You might offer a nonspecific remark such as, "I'm sorry to hear that." But if they clarify, "I feel overwhelmed and anxious because I have a big presentation tomorrow, and my heart is racing," you can offer more targeted support, such as suggesting relaxation techniques or delivering words of encouragement.

Expressing emotions constructively is another crucial part of emotional literacy. This means articulating your feelings honestly and respectfully without criticizing or assaulting your spouse. Instead of expressing, "You always make me angry," try, "I feel angry when I feel unheard during our disagreements." This shift in vocabulary focuses on your own experience, opening the door for a more constructive discourse.

Developing emotional literacy is a constant process of self-discovery and mutual understanding. Here are some methods to assist you and your spouse in increasing your emotional vocabulary and understanding:

- The Emotion Wheel: This visual tool displays a broad spectrum of emotions, grouped by intensity and relationship to one another. Use the wheel to highlight certain feelings and improve your emotional vocabulary. For example, if you're feeling "bad," the Emotion Wheel can help you distinguish whether you're experiencing sadness, anger, fear, or a combination of feelings.

- Journaling: Regularly track your emotional experiences in a journal. Describe the scenario, your emotions, physical sensations related to those emotions, and any thoughts or beliefs that arose. This practice helps you uncover patterns and triggers, enhancing your self-awareness. For instance, you might find that you tend to feel worried and angry in the evenings when you're exhausted or that specific topics of conversation elicit feelings of melancholy or rage.

- Feelings Check-In: Schedule regular "feelings check-ins" with your partner. Create a secure area to share your emotional experiences without judgment. Use "I" statements to communicate your feelings and carefully listen to your partner's perspective. This can mean setting aside 15 minutes each week to discuss how you're feeling, what obstacles you're facing, and what support you need from each other.

- Empathy Exercises: Engage in activities that promote empathy, such as reading fiction, watching documentaries, or helping in your community. These experiences can help you comprehend and respect diverse perspectives and emotional experiences. Venturing beyond your bubble and connecting with diverse worldviews can help you acquire deeper compassion and empathy for your partner's sentiments.

- Seek feedback: Ask your spouse for guidance on your communication style. Are you clearly expressing your emotions? Are you listening intently to their perspective? Open and honest comments can help you enhance your communication skills and strengthen your emotional connection. For example, you might question your partner, "When I express anger, do you feel heard and understood, or do you feel attacked?"

Developing emotional literacy is a constant process, but the rewards are worth the effort. Investing in this ability teaches you the tools to negotiate conflict constructively, deepen your connection, and build a more meaningful and resilient relationship.

Key Points

- Emotions function as messengers, offering vital information about your inner condition, desires, and boundaries.

- Unexpressed emotions don't disappear; they might reemerge in undesirable ways, like anger concealing fear or sadness.

- Developing emotional literacy entails increasing your language beyond phrases like "happy" or "sad."

- Connecting emotions to physical sensations helps you detect and understand your emotional state more quickly.

- Expressing emotions productively entails clear, polite communication without condemning your spouse.

Self-Reflection Questions

1. What other feelings may be present when you are angry? Do you feel any underlying fear, hurt, or frustration?

_____

_____

_____

_____

_____

2. How do you usually express sadness? Do you allow yourself to experience it entirely, or do you repress or discard it?

_____

_____

_____

_____

_____

3. What physical feelings come with different emotions for you? Is anxiety manifested as a racing heart, or is guilt felt as a knot in your throat?

_____

_____

_____

_____

_____

4. How do you usually express your emotions to your partner? Do you express them plainly and bluntly or use hints or subtle cues?

_____

_____

_____

_____

5. When your partner displays their emotions, how do you react? Do you listen with empathy and acknowledge their feelings, or are you defensive or dismissive?

_____

_____

Chapter 5: Mastering the Art of Communication

"The single biggest problem in communication is the illusion that it has taken place." - George Bernard Shaw

Shaw's statements illustrate a typical problem in human interaction: we often feel we've communicated effectively when, in reality, our message has become lost in translation. Mastering the art of communication, especially during conflict, needs more than just stating our opinions; it demands attentive listening, clear expression, and a willingness to bridge the gap between our perspectives.

Think of communication as a dance, a subtle interplay of give and take. Each couple must play their part, listening carefully and expressing themselves clearly to create a smooth flow. When one partner dominates the dance floor, stepping on toes and ignoring cues, the rhythm falters, and detachment sets in.

Active listening is the cornerstone of this dance. It includes more than just hearing your spouse's words; it demands a sincere effort to understand their perspective and to grasp the feelings and requirements underneath their words. Active listening demands presence, curiosity, and a willingness to entirely suppress your internal commentary to hear what your partner is saying.

Imagine your partner, frustrated over "no helping hands" around the house. An active listener can reply, "I sense that you're feeling overwhelmed and unappreciated. Can you tell me more about what's contributing to that feeling?" This response demonstrates that you're paying attention, caring about them, and willing to get the point they're trying to make.

Compare this with an inconsiderate reply like, "Well, I'm tired too, and I work all day." This response invalidates your partner's emotions and shuts down further discussion. It's like turning up the music and ignoring your partner's cues on the dance floor, leading to isolation and hatred.

Active listening incorporates both verbal and nonverbal cues. Maintain eye contact, nod your head to demonstrate engagement, and use verbal affirmations like "uh-huh" or "I understand" to signal your attention. Reflect on what you've heard to verify you've comprehended correctly: "So, it seems like you're feeling frustrated because you feel like you're bearing most of the household responsibilities. Is that right?"

Avoid interrupting your spouse, especially if you disagree with their perspective. Allow them to express themselves fully before sharing your own opinions and feelings. This communicates respect and offers a safe atmosphere for open communication.

Clear expression forms the second side of this communication dance. It entails explaining your thoughts and feelings in a way your spouse can quickly understand. This demands clarity, conciseness, and a focus on "I" assertions.

Instead of saying, "You always leave your clothes on the floor," try, "I feel frustrated when I see clothes on the floor because it makes me feel like our shared space isn't respected." This "I" statement reveals your feelings without accusing or abusing your spouse, making them more open to your message.

Choose your words carefully, avoiding generalizations and harsh rhetoric. Replace accusing remarks like, "You never listen to me," with concrete examples: "When I was talking about my day earlier, I noticed you were looking at your phone. That made me feel like I wasn't important to you."

Pay attention to your tone of voice and body language. Even the most carefully thought-out words might lose significance if conveyed with a harsh tone or dismissive posture. Strive for a calm and respectful approach, especially when feeling bad.

Mastering the art of communication involves practice and a willingness to learn from your failures. Here are some resources to assist you and your partner strengthen your communication skills:

- Mirroring: This approach entails reflecting on your partner's statement to ensure you've gotten their message accurately. For example, your partner might say, "I feel overwhelmed with all the household chores." You could reply with, "So, you're feeling overwhelmed with the amount of housework?" This simple reflection simplifies their message and reveals that you're attentively listening.

- Validation: Validation is noticing and respecting your partner's emotions, even if you disagree with what they're saying. This doesn't imply you condone their behavior, but it indicates that you respect their feelings and are eager to understand their experience. For instance, if your partner feels upset about a disagreement, you should reply with, "I get why you're angry right now. It makes sense why you would feel that way given the situation."

- Time-Outs: Agree on a "time-out" signal that either of you can utilize when feeling overwhelmed or swamped during a debate. This allows you to pause, cool down, and return to the topic when you're both more receptive to communication.

- Active Listening Exercises: Engage in activities that develop your active listening skills. One practice involves one person speaking for a fixed amount of time while the other listens intently without interrupting. The listener then describes what they heard, and the speaker offers feedback on the accuracy of their comprehension.

- Communication Skills Workshops or Therapy: Consider attending a communication skills program or seeking couples therapy to enhance your communication skills. A therapist can offer individualized feedback and strategies to help you handle communication issues and build relationships.

Mastering the art of communication is a fixed task, a dance that needs continuous refinement and adaptability.

Active Listening: Hearing Beyond the Words

Think of a discussion as a tennis match. One person serves, the other returns, and the volley continues back and forth. But what if one player continuously misses the ball, or worse, stands with their back turned, refusing to participate? Communication falls out, irritation grows, and the game ends in resentment. Active listening is crucial to keeping the game alive, a skill that converts discussion from a competitive sport to a collaborative dance.

It's far more than just hearing your spouse's words; it's a deep dive into their world, an authentic effort to comprehend their viewpoint, their emotions, and the needs stimulating their words. It involves presence, curiosity, and a desire to quiet your internal critique to digest what your partner is talking about.

Suppose your partner expresses anger about a recent family event. An active listener can react with, "It sounds like that gathering was challenging for you. Can you tell me more about what happened?" This response says you're present, you care, and you're ready to hear their story.

Contrast this with a dismissive reaction like, "Oh, you always complain about my family." This shuts down communication and invalidates their emotions. It's like turning your back on the tennis court, refusing to engage in the volley.

Active listening incorporates both verbal and nonverbal cues. Maintain eye contact, nod to demonstrate engagement, and use verbal affirmations like "uh-huh" or "I see" to signal your attention. Reflect on what you've heard for clarification: "So, it sounds like you felt uncomfortable at the gathering since my aunt kept making jokes about your job. Is that correct?"

Avoid interrupting, even if you disagree. Allow your partner to express themselves fully before adding your take. This communicates respect and offers a haven for open communication. It's like waiting for the ball to pass the net before trying to rebound it.

Here are some practical ways to reinforce your active listening abilities during conflict:

- Focus on Understanding, Not Rebuttal: When your spouse speaks, avoid the desire to develop your answer or counter-argument. Instead, focus on actually understanding their viewpoint. Ask questions for clarification like, "Can you give me a scenario of what you mean?" or "How did that make you feel?"

- Pay Attention to Nonverbal Signals: Observe your partner's body language, facial expressions, and tone of voice. These nonverbal clues tend to convey more than words alone. If your partner's voice is tense or their arms are crossed, they might feel anxious or defensive. Acknowledge these cues and alter your conversation accordingly.

- Repeat and Interpret: Periodically repeat what you've heard to verify you're on the same page. "So, you're offended because I neglected our anniversary. Is that correct?" This shows your partner that you're actively listening and attempting to comprehend their point of view.

- Validate Their Emotions: Even if you disagree with your partner's viewpoint, identify and validate their emotions. "I understand that you're feeling upset right now. It makes sense that you would feel that way." This demonstrates respect and offers a sense of safety for your spouse to express themselves openly.

- Practice Patience: Active listening needs patience, especially during heated debates. Resist the desire to interrupt or jump to conclusions. Give your partner the time and space they need to express themselves fully.

Active listening is essential for de-escalating conflict and developing more robust connections. It turns arguments from battles to be won into opportunities for reconciliation and growth.

Speaking Your Truth with Clarity and Compassion

Visualize telling the truth as a tightrope walk. It demands balance, precision, and an awareness of your stance. On one side lies the pit of silence, where unexpressed needs and bottled-up emotions fester and build hatred. On the other side yawns the pit of violence, where anger outbursts and bitter words erode trust and create distance from one another.

Walking on this tightrope with competence and ease requires clarity and compassion, a delicate blend of firmness and compassion. It's about expressing your feelings openly and genuinely while still respecting your partner's viewpoint and maintaining the connection you share.

Imagine a couple arguing about how to spend a free Saturday. One partner prefers to spend the day at home, while the other yearns for an adventurous day out. Without clear communication, this disparity may become an annoying stalemate. But with open and compassionate communication, the conversation could turn out like this: "I appreciate your willingness to explore that new hiking trail, but I honestly need some downtime this weekend. Could we create a compromise that honors both our needs?"

This strategy clearly presents your intention while appreciating your partner's perspective. It opens the door for a collaborative solution rather than a win-lose clash of wills.

Telling the truth with clarity starts with understanding the essence of your message. What do you genuinely want to communicate? What requirements or concerns lay beneath your immediate reaction? Strip away any blame or judgment and focus on articulating your own experience.

Instead of stating, "You always make me feel ignored when you're on your phone during dinner," try, "I feel disconnected when I'm trying to chat with you because you're always on your phone. It makes me feel like I'm not significant to you." This shift in vocabulary focuses on your sentiments and invites your spouse to comprehend your perspective.

Choose your words wisely. Avoid generalizations and harsh language that can create defensiveness. Replace accusing remarks like, "You never listen to me," with concrete examples: "When I was talking about my day earlier, I noticed you were looking at your phone. That made me feel like I wasn't a priority."

Pay attention to your tone of voice and body language. Even the most carefully selected words might lose their effect if given with a harsh tone or disdainful posture. Strive for a calm and respectful approach, especially when expressing bad feelings. Maintain eye contact, adopt a kind tone, and maintain your body language open and responsive.

Assertive communication creates a balance between passivity and assertiveness. It's about clearly and boldly communicating your wants and boundaries while respecting your partner's rights and viewpoints. It's not about winning or losing but finding a solution that works for both of you.

Here are some strategies for assertive communication:

- Use "I" comments: As discussed previously, "I" statements focus on your personal experience rather than criticizing your partner. They allow you to express your sentiments and desires without triggering defensiveness. For example, instead of expressing, "You're always late," try, "I feel anxious when you're late because I worry that something might have happened."

- Set clear boundaries: Boundaries determine your limits and expectations in the partnership. Communicate your boundaries clearly and politely, and be prepared to enforce them. For instance, if you require quiet time in the evenings to de-stress, convey this need to your partner and ask for their cooperation in respecting your boundaries.

- Practice active listening: Assertive communication isn't only about expressing yourself; it's also about actively listening to your partner's perspective. Please pay attention to their words, tone of voice, and body language. Reflect on what you've heard to ensure you comprehend their point of view.

- Use the "broken record" technique: If your partner tries to divert or dismiss your concerns, gently repeat your message using the same terminology. This strategy communicates your dedication to your demands and boundaries without escalating the conflict.

- Seek compromise: Assertive communication doesn't mean always getting your way. Be open to negotiating and compromise to discover solutions for you and your partner. This can require discussing different options, considering each other's priorities, and finding a medium ground that suits both of you.

Speaking your truth with clarity and compassion is a skill that takes practice. It's about finding a way to talk, acknowledging your needs, and communicating with empathy and respect.

Key Points

- Active listening is more than hearing sounds; it involves authentically trying to comprehend your partner's viewpoint and emotions.

- Repeating what you've heard implies that you fully understand your partner's message and are interested.

- Open communication means sharing your thoughts and feelings in a way your spouse can easily comprehend, utilizing specific examples, and avoiding generalizations.

- "I" statements articulate your sentiments and wants without blaming or assaulting your partner, making them more open to your words.

- Assertive communication means confidently expressing your demands and boundaries while respecting your partner's standpoint and finding a balance between indifference and violence.

Self-Reflection Questions

1. When your partner talks, do you really listen to understand, or do you already plan to respond in your head?

_____
_____
_____
_____
_____

2. On what occasions do you interrupt your partner during conversations, especially disagreements?

_____
_____
_____
_____
_____

3. Would you rather use generalizations like "always" or "never" when discussing your partner's behavior?

_____
_____
_____
_____
_____

4. How often do you express your needs and wants openly, or do you rely on hints and hope your spouse finds out about them?

_____
_____
_____
_____
_____

5. When you disagree with your partner, do you aim for a win-win solution, or do you focus on proving your point and getting what you want?

Chapter 6: Creating a Safe Space for Vulnerability

"Vulnerability is not winning or losing; it's having the courage to show up and be seen when we have no control over the outcome." - Brené Brown

Vulnerability, as Brown defines it, is the willingness to show our true selves, even when doing so feels questionable or dangerous. It is the cornerstone of strong connection and trust in close relationships. It's the readiness to let our guard down, to communicate our anxieties and fears, and to let our partner see us for who we really are—flaws and all.

Picture a medieval castle with high walls and strong gates to keep its occupants safe. Although these shields provide a feeling of safety, they often lead to loneliness. Lowering the drawbridge, opening the gates, and letting someone else inside the inner sanctum of our hearts are necessary for a genuine relationship.

Building a sanctuary—where both partners feel safe enough to express their deepest aspirations, dreams, and anxieties without worrying about criticism or rejection—is analogous to creating a safe space for vulnerability in a partnership. Because it fosters open communication, empathy, and a desire to overcome obstacles, this haven offers a basis for positively handling conflict.

Building trust is the first step in creating this sanctuary. Trust is a conviction in your partner's dependability, honesty, and good intentions developed over time by consistent behavior and honest conversation; it is not blind faith. It's the assurance that your significant other will tactfully handle your vulnerabilities, react with compassion, and avoid using your secrets as leverage when you argue.

Being open and honest is one method of building trust. Even if doing it makes you feel uncomfortable, be honest and transparent about your feelings and views. Refrain from denying or downplaying your feelings, as this might cause distrust and distance. Listen empathetically and validate your partner's experience when they disclose their weaknesses. Demonstrate your appreciation for their honesty and your readiness to treat them kindly.

Respect is another essential component in establishing a secure space. Respect entails appreciating your partner's limits, values, and viewpoints—even if they diverge from yours. It involves being considerate and courteous to them even when disagreeing. Steer clear of insults, name-calling, and verbal or emotional abuse. These actions destroy trust and foster an atmosphere of uneasiness and anxiety.

Consistency is essential when creating a secure atmosphere. Your words and deeds must be consistent. If you commit to maintaining your partner's trust, keep your word. Show your dedication by your actions if you say you want to establish a safe environment for vulnerability. Your partner finds it difficult to feel comfortable disclosing their vulnerabilities when inconsistency breeds confusion and undermines trust.

Any relationship will inevitably involve mending rifts. Disagreements, miscommunications, and cruel remarks can undermine trust. To mend these ruptures, you must accept responsibility for your actions, acknowledge the pain caused, and extend a heartfelt apology. This also entails acknowledging your partner's pain and listening to their stories.

After a break, forgiveness is essential to restoring trust. Forgiveness is a deliberate decision to relinquish grudges and move on; it does not imply endorsing cruel actions. It's a self-care practice that enables you to recover and reestablish a relationship with your partner.

The goal of creating a safe space for vulnerability is to establish an atmosphere where both partners feel comfortable letting their guard down and sharing their true selves without worrying about criticism or rejection.

Building Trust and Safety in Your Relationship

Consider trust to be the cornerstone of a relationship, the basis for closeness, bonding, and resiliency. A partnership without trust is like a house on sand, ready to fall apart at the first hint of a storm. In turn, safety is the refuge this home offers, where both partners can be themselves without worrying about criticism or rejection.

Safety and trust are even more critical when there is a dispute. Disagreements are inevitable, resulting in uncomfortable feelings, vulnerabilities, and a sense of security. Couples may confidently navigate these choppy waters in relationships where trust and safety thrive because they know their bond is strong enough to endure the waves of conflict.

Suppose a couple is struggling financially. This problem could lead to blame, accusations, and defensiveness in a relationship without trust. However, in a relationship based on safety and trust, the couple can approach the problem cooperatively, freely discussing their worries, fears, and possible solutions. They have faith that their spouse will cooperate to find a solution that works for both of them, and they are sure that their relationship is strong enough to withstand any challenges.

It takes perseverance and dedication to foster the relationship to establish safety and trust. It must be watered, weeded, and fertilized regularly to maintain growth and vitality, much like a garden.

Here are some specific strategies for fostering safety and trust in your relationship:

- Put Honesty and Transparency First: Trust relies on honesty. Even when it seems challenging, try to communicate honestly and openly. Talk to your spouse about your feelings, ideas, and experiences, and urge them to do the same. Concealed or minimized information should be avoided, which undermines confidence and breeds mistrust.

- Keep Your Promises: Don't renege on a commitment, no matter how minor. Make sure you pledge to stop by the grocery store on your way home. Keep your word if you and your partner decide to go to a social function. When you're consistent in your actions, you establish dependability and show your spouse you are dependable.

- Respect Boundaries: Everybody has boundaries, which are indistinguishable lines that indicate their expectations and limits. Even if your partner's boundaries are different from your own, respect them. Be willing to listen, make any adjustments, and express your boundaries courteously and straightforwardly. Respecting limits shows you respect your partner's independence and put their comfort and welfare first.

- Engage in Active Listening: Active listening means paying attention and comprehending your partner's viewpoint, even if you disagree. Observe their body language, tone of voice, and words. Repeat what you have heard to ensure you fully understand their message. This shows consideration and establishes a secure environment for candid dialogue.

- Provide Support and Validation: Show empathy and validation to your spouse when they disclose their vulnerabilities. Remind them that you are there for them, hear them, and comprehend their situation. Steer clear of criticism or judgment since this can stifle dialogue and foster feelings of insecurity.

- Spend Quality Time Together: Schedule time for pursuits that deepen your bond and foster experiences you can share. This could include weekend trips, dating nights, or just spending time together at home, laughing, talking, and enjoying each other's company. Shared experiences strengthen your relationship and foster connection.

- Express regret and forgiveness: Everyone makes errors. Acknowledge the harm that you have caused, accept responsibility for your actions, and sincerely apologize to your spouse. Practice forgiving your partner when they apologize. Forgiveness is a deliberate decision to relinquish grudges and move on; it does not imply endorsing cruel actions.

- Seek Professional Help When Needed: Don't be afraid to get professional assistance if you need help establishing trust or a safe space in your relationship. A therapist can offer direction and assistance in overcoming obstacles, improving communication, and fortifying your relationship.

When you have built safety and trust, you can handle conflict with confidence because you know that your relationship will weather the storms of dispute and emerge stronger on the other side.

Repairing Ruptures and Rebuilding Connection

Consider your relationship as a delicately and lovingly crafted piece of pottery. Conflict can lead to fractures and cracks in this structure, much like an unintentional drop. Even while these flaws could appear to be permanent harm, restoration can return the item to its prior splendor while frequently enhancing its strength and durability.

Mending interpersonal rifts requires a gentle touch, vulnerability, empathy, and a sincere desire to reestablish connection. It also involves expressing genuine regret, accepting responsibility for your actions, and admitting the damage you have caused. Even if you don't completely comprehend or agree with your partner's point of view, it's still important to listen to their suffering and validate their experience.

Suppose that a couple is fighting over a missed anniversary. While one spouse feels defensive and misunderstood, the other feels hurt and ignored. The connection between them is strained, and the air crackles with tension. The partner who forgot the anniversary could remark, "I'm so sorry I forgot our anniversary," to mend this rift. I'm sorry for disappointing you; I understand how much it matters to you. Could you elaborate on your feelings for me?

This apology expresses regret for the harm caused, accepts responsibility for the mistake, and demonstrates an interest in learning about the partner's experience. It allows for a more in-depth discussion, allowing the hurt partner to express their emotions and feel understood and supported.

Repair attempts provide immediate relief and stop additional harm, making them the emotional equivalent of first aid. They express a wish to reestablish contact with your spouse and defuse tension. These efforts can be made in a variety of ways:

- Expressing regret verbally: "I apologize. I had no intention of hurting you."
- Affectionate touch: A warm hug or a soft hand on their arm are examples of affectionate contact.
- Empathy statements include "I can see that I upset you."
- Accepting accountability: "I acknowledge that I overreacted."
- Compromise proposals: "Let's find a way to work this out together."

These modest actions can significantly impact stress and create a space for more in-depth dialogue and healing.

After a disagreement, both parties must be committed to reestablishing their relationship. It's about putting empathy and understanding above defensiveness and blaming. The following techniques can assist you in reestablishing communication following a conflict:

- Take a break: Agree to end the conversation if emotions escalate. This lets you both relax, work through your emotions, and return to the conversation with a more lucid perspective.

- Listen with empathy: When you're prepared to start talking again, concentrate on hearing your partner's point of view with compassion. Even if you disagree with their story, try to comprehend it. To ensure you understand their viewpoint, repeat what you have heard.

- Express your sentiments: Using "I" phrases, express your wants and feelings about the conflict without blaming your spouse.

- Establish common ground: Seek for points of agreement or similar viewpoints. This might let you know you're on the same team and help you reestablish a connection.

- Offer and accept forgiveness: Forgiveness can be a powerful tool for rebuilding trust and healing. It is a deliberate decision to let go of anger and move on, and it does not imply endorsing cruel actions. Be prepared to accept your partner's forgiveness and extend it to them.

- Show love and kindness: Even small acts of gratitude and compassion can significantly impact reestablishing a connection. To let your partner know you value and are dedicated to the relationship, give them a hug, a compliment, or a kind gesture.

- Establish a reconciliation routine: Establish a ritual you and your spouse might follow to signal the conclusion of a disagreement and reestablish your relationship. This could be a simple act of love and devotion, a special dinner, or a shared pastime.

Understanding that disagreement is unavoidable but need not define your relationship is the first step in mending rifts and reestablishing the connection.

Key Points

- Vulnerability means showing your spouse your true self, flaws and all.

- Trust must be established via open communication and consistent action to create a haven for vulnerability.

- Establishing a sense of safety requires respecting your partner's boundaries, values, and opinions—even when you disagree.

- To mend ruptures, you must admit wrongdoing, accept responsibility, sincerely apologize, and validate your partner's viewpoint.

- You can heal and reestablish a connection by consciously choosing to forgive, let go of grudges, and move on.

Self-Reflection Questions

1. To what extent do you feel at ease discussing your worries and fears with your significant other? Do you usually put up barriers or hold back to protect yourself?

_____
_____
_____
_____

2. How do you usually react when your partner exposes their vulnerabilities? Do you condemn or brush off their emotions, or do you listen to them with compassion and give support?

_____
_____
_____
_____

3. How do you resolve conflicts? Do you continue to show consideration for your partner's viewpoint, or do you use insults or personal assaults instead?

_____
_____
_____
_____

4. How do you usually mend the rift caused by hurting your partner? Do you accept responsibility for the harm done, sidestep the problem, or do you criticize them?

_____
_____
_____
_____

5. When your significant other hurts you, how quickly do you forgive them? Do you intentionally

try to let go and move on, or do you harbor resentment?

_____
_____
_____
_____
_____

Part 3
<u>Transforming Conflict into Connection</u>

Chapter 7: Navigating Common Conflict Scenarios

"Most people do not listen with the intent to understand; they listen with the intent to reply." - Stephen R. Covey

Covey's statements draw attention to a typical communication blunder: We frequently enter discussions, mainly at odds, with preconceived notions about our agendas and counterarguments. This propensity might intensify rather than resolve disagreement and obstruct comprehension. To successfully handle conflict situations, we need to develop a backup plan based on empathy, attentive listening, and an attempt to identify points of agreement.

Conflict in a relationship that recurs is similar to shabby paths in a forest. The path becomes more ingrained with each repetition, making deviation more difficult. You'll have to take another path to venture off the beaten route to find ideas and new solutions.

The division of household chores is one typical conflict scenario. One spouse often feels stressed and overwhelmed in relationships, while the other feels unappreciated or misunderstood. This disparity might result in anger, annoyance, and injustice.

Consider a relationship in which one partner works full-time and the other takes care of the kids at home. While the working partner may feel undervalued for their long working hours and financial support, the stay-at-home partner may feel overburdened by the constant demands of childcare and housekeeping. This situation frequently manifests in subtle ways, such as a mocking remark about a neglected task, a sigh of frustration as dishes pile up, or a retreat from closeness brought on by fatigue and contempt.

To resolve this dispute, both couples must value their partner's efforts and recognize their contributions. The stay-at-home partner may thank the working partner for providing financial stability, and the working partner may thank the stay-at-home partner for their commitment to the family.

Next, discuss the division of labor openly and truthfully. Steer clear of generalizations or accusing rhetoric. Instead, explicitly state your needs and concentrate on concrete instances. "I feel overwhelmed with the amount of housework and childcare I handle," the stay-at-home partner may respond by saying, "Is it possible for us to divide these duties more fairly?" The working partner may reply, "I know you're feeling overburdened. Although I would be willing to assist more around the house, I also require some relaxation after work. Can we arrange a timetable that suits us both?

By working together, both partners may communicate their requirements and come up with an equitable solution. To account for each partner's contributions, this could entail making a chore chart, contracting out certain work, or just changing expectations.

Money-related conflicts are another regular incidence. Money is more than just a tool for trade; it has emotional significance and stands for strength, freedom, and security. Deeply ingrained fears and phobias can be triggered by disagreements over spending patterns, savings objectives, or financial priorities.

Consider a couple with disparate spending habits. While one partner enjoys spending money on pleasures and instant satisfaction, the other partner prioritizes saving for the future. Conflict may result from this mismatch in values, with one spouse feeling constrained and the other careless.

Both couples must first assess their financial relationships to resolve this problem. What are your priorities and values in terms of money? What emotional connection to money do you have, and what prompts your spending? You can talk to your partner more effectively after you better understand your financial situation.

Set up frequent money dates to discuss your financial objectives, worries, and tactics. Approach these discussions with a cooperative and accommodating mindset. Don't criticize one another's spending patterns. Instead, identify solutions that complement your long-term objectives and shared values.

This could entail establishing financial boundaries, creating a budget, or consulting a financial counselor. The key is approaching money conversations with openness, deference, and a readiness to compromise.

Conflict frequently arises from parenting choices, particularly when spouses have divergent ideologies or approaches. Disagreements about extracurricular activities, education, or discipline might weaken a cohesive front.

Imagine a couple that can't agree on how to discipline their kid. While one partner likes a rigid approach, the other favors a more liberal and kind one. Conflict may result from this disparity in strategy, with each partner feeling undercut or abandoned.

In order to resolve this disagreement, both couples must acknowledge that there is no one "right" approach to parenting. What works for one family may not work for another, and different children react differently to different methods. Parenting conversations must be approached with an open mind and a desire to share knowledge.

Schedule frequent parenting meetings to discuss your parenting views, difficulties, and tactics. Concentrate on identifying points of agreement and developing a method that works for you both. This could entail consulting a therapist, attending parenting classes, or reading parenting literature together.

Even if you argue privately, the goal is to show your kids that you are all on the same page. This uniformity makes your children feel more secure, which also improves your relationship.

Individual requirements and preferences can lead to recurring disagreements. One partner may constantly need physical touch, while the other shows their love by helping others. While one person thrives on routine and predictability, the other may value spontaneity more. Even though these differences are not always troublesome, if they are not handled positively, they may cause conflict.

The secret is acknowledging and valuing these distinctions and figuring out how to meet one another's demands without compromising your own. This could entail reaching a compromise, coming up with solutions, or valuing your partner's distinct approach to showing love and navigating the world.

For instance, one partner may deliberately try to start hugs or cuddling more frequently if the other partner wants more regular physical intimacy. The other partner might give in to random surprises or adventures if one partner enjoys unpredictability while still keeping their daily schedule consistent and structured.

When dealing with these typical conflict situations, you must be willing to venture outside of your comfort zone and try new things. It involves identifying the patterns that lead to conflict, having courteous and clear communication, and coming up with solutions that respect the needs and values of both parties.

Money Matters: Resolving Financial Disputes

Money. The word alone has the power to evoke a variety of feelings, from tension and worry to comfort and security. Financial arguments frequently spark relationships, bringing to light more severe problems with priorities, values, and power dynamics. It takes open conversation, respect for one another, and a desire to establish a common ground to become an expert at settling financial disagreements.

Imagine a couple fighting over a new purchase. While one partner is upset about the needless spending, the other purchased a new device. This seemingly straightforward argument may conceal deeper issues: one partner prioritizes experiences and instant gratification, while the other places more importance on saving and financial stability. The conflict risks becoming recurrent if these underlying values are not addressed.

The first step towards successfully resolving financial issues is to recognize the emotional burden that money bears. Many people associate stability and safety with economic security. Financial difficulties might trigger anxiety and vulnerability. Your partner's responses to money may be influenced by their values or past experiences.

Instead of criticizing your partner's decisions, approach money conversations with empathy and inquiry, trying to grasp their point of view. Ask open-ended questions rather than offering criticism: "I saw that you purchased a new device. Could you elaborate on your reasoning for making that purchase? This method allows for a deeper understanding by asking your spouse to explain their reasons.

Next, look at how you relate to money. Which financial priorities do you have? Do you place more importance on finding balance, having fun in the here and now, or saving for the future? What causes you to spend money? Do you tend to overspend when stressed or attempting to satisfy an emotional need?

Knowing your financial trends and emotional triggers can help you and your partner converse more successfully. It can also aid in the development of plans and the identification of possible conflict spots.

Establishing a shared financial vision is essential to coordinating your objectives and averting conflicts. Plan frequent "money dates" to discuss your goals, worries, and priorities related to money. This could entail establishing long-term objectives, such as retirement savings or purchasing a home. It also entails discussing more immediate objectives like organizing a trip or making a significant purchase.

Seek out areas of agreement and approach these discussions with a collaborative mindset. This could entail reaching a compromise, developing original ideas, or respecting your partner's viewpoint.

Couples frequently fight over budgeting, particularly when one partner feels constrained. Reframe a budget as a tool for accomplishing your mutual financial objectives rather than as a limitation. A budget gives you direction, makes it easier to keep tabs on your expenses, and allows you to make thoughtful decisions.

Together, develop a budget while making sure each partner feels heard. This could entail tracking income and expenses with a spreadsheet, a budgeting tool, or a notebook. Sort your expenditures, find places where you can save, and set aside money for personal and group objectives.

Regularly review your budget and make any necessary adjustments. Honor accomplishments and resolve any issues amicably and cooperatively.

Disparities in spending patterns frequently exacerbate conflict. While one partner may like to preserve money, the other may prefer to spend it on adventures. Due to these discrepancies, one spouse may feel deprived, and the other may be evaluated, which can lead to conflict.

To solve this, recognize and appreciate one another's spending habits. Understand that everyone experiences joy differently. Find a balance rather than attempting to alter your partner's behavior.

This could entail establishing personal spending caps, setting up a "fun fund" for luxuries, or being transparent about priorities and spending decisions. The aim is to find a structure that enables both parties to feel fulfilled and financially secure.

Financial disagreements frequently expose deeper problems with control and power. One couple may feel more in control regarding monetary matters while the other feels ignored. This disparity may lead to hatred.

To address this, aim for equity and openness when making financial decisions. Make certain that both couples can access financial data and participate in important financial choices. This could entail open conversation regarding all financial matters, shared access to financial documents, or joint bank accounts.

If one partner manages the majority of the money, plan frequent meetings to discuss the budget and financial objectives. This guarantees that each partner feels knowledgeable and equipped to make decisions that support their common goal.

A change in viewpoint is necessary to settle financial disagreements. Reframe money to accomplish your shared goals and create a safe future rather than as a cause of contention.

Parenting Conflicts: Finding Common Ground

Relationship conflict frequently arises due to parenting, an incredibly joyful and inevitably challenging journey. Conflicts about screen time, education, discipline, and other parenting issues can strain a relationship, make it seem less cohesive, and make both parties feel ignored and dissatisfied. It takes open communication, respect for one another, and a readiness to put your kids' welfare ahead of your preferences to find common ground.

Imagine a couple fighting about when to put their child to bed. While one partner wants a more flexible schedule, the other insists on a rigid bedtime of 8 p.m. This seemingly little argument may reveal deeper parenting ideologies: one couple favors flexibility and responsiveness to the child's specific needs, while the other values structure and consistency. The dispute risks turning into a power struggle if these fundamental beliefs are not addressed, leaving the child in the middle.

Understanding that there is no one-size-fits-all method of childrearing is the first step in successfully resolving parenting disputes. What suits one household may not suit another. Every child has requirements, temperament, and developmental path. If you approach parenting conversations with humility and an open mind, you can learn from one another and develop ideas that are best for your child's welfare.

Set up frequent "parenting meetings" to discuss your parenting views, difficulties, and techniques. These gatherings offer a specific setting for candid dialogue and group problem-solving. Select a period when you are unhurried and at ease. Approach the discussion respectfully instead of judging your partner's viewpoints.

During these sessions, discuss particular parenting issues and consider various strategies. For instance, discuss your opinions on good discipline techniques if you differ in discipline. Examine several parenting philosophies, such as authoritarian, permissive, and authoritative, and decide which best suits your child's needs and ideals.

Keep in mind that children's sense of safety and well-being depend heavily on consistency. Diverse parenting philosophies are healthy, but whenever feasible, present a unified front. This entails establishing clear expectations for your kids, supporting one another's choices—even if you don't agree on them in private—and deciding on a general strategy to discipline.

When disagreements occur, refrain from disparaging or criticizing your spouse in front of your kids. This may undermine their confidence and make them feel uneasy. Instead, stop the conversation and return to the matter later when you can speak politely and quietly.

Effective co-parenting necessitates making concessions and devising solutions that benefit you and your kids. Finding a middle ground between various tactics, combining your parenting styles, or agreeing to disagree on some matters while putting on a constant front could all be part of this.

Setting a general bedtime range and allowing for some flexibility based on the child's unique needs and circumstances could be a compromise if, for instance, one couple prefers a more flexible approach. In contrast, the other prefers a regimented nighttime ritual.

Co-parenting requires teamwork, so keep that in mind. Celebrate your parenting accomplishments together, encourage one another, and support one another's choices. In addition to helping your kids, this cooperative approach improves your relationship as a couple.

The following resources will assist you in successfully resolving parenting disputes and co-parenting:

1. Parenting Books and Resources: Read books and articles about child development, parenting approaches, and efficient methods of discipline. This shared knowledge can provide a common vocabulary and structure for discussing parenting difficulties.

2. Parenting Classes or Workshops: Take part in parenting classes or workshops with your partner. These provide a controlled setting for acquiring new abilities, exchanging stories with other parents, and receiving expert assistance.

3. Therapist or Counselor: If you're having trouble resolving ongoing parenting disputes or finding common ground, you might want advice from a therapist or counselor. An impartial third person

can provide support, communication, and the development of successful co-parenting techniques.

4. "Parenting Dates": Arrange frequent "parenting dates" to discuss your objectives, difficulties, and achievements. During these dates, you can bond, brainstorm ideas, and commemorate your common parenting journey.

5. Empathy and Active Listening: Show empathy and active listening when having conversations on parenting. Try comprehending your partner's viewpoint, acknowledging their emotions, and politely communicating your needs and concerns.

Even though they can be difficult, parenting disputes present chances for development and closer bonds.

Key Points

- Differing values and priorities, such as one partner prioritizing experiences while the other values conserving, frequently cause recurring problems.

- To effectively navigate financial arguments, you and your partner must acknowledge the emotional burden that money bears.

- Open conversation about financial objectives, worries, and spending patterns produces transparency and decreases the possibility of misunderstandings.

- By developing a unified financial vision that includes both short-term and long-term objectives, priorities can be aligned, and future disputes can be avoided.

- Resolving disparities in financial decision-making fosters equality and keeps interpersonal anger from growing.

Self-Reflection Questions

1. What feelings come to mind when you think of money? Do you consider it freedom, worry, security, or something else?

_____

_____

_____

_____

2. What would you say about your spending patterns? Which would you prefer—saving for the future or enjoying the present?

_____

_____

_____

_____

3. How do you and your partner usually resolve financial disputes? Do you tend to shut down or get defensive when communicating, or do you talk politely and openly?

_____

_____

_____

_____

_____

4. Do you share a financial vision with your partner? Have you talked about your long-term financial priorities and goals?

_____

_____

_____

_____

_____

5. In your partnership, who is in charge of handling money matters? Do you believe that each partner has an equal voice regarding financial decisions?

_____

_____

Chapter 8: The Art of Compromise and Negotiation

"Compromise is the best and cheapest lawyer." - Robert Louis Stevenson

Stevenson's remarks highlight the value of reaching a compromise in conflict resolution, a talent crucial in the private sphere of relationships and legal conflicts. The foundation of effective conflict resolution is compromise, the skill of coming up with solutions that all parties can agree on. The link between two seemingly incompatible coasts enables partners to arrive at a place that meets their needs.

Imagine a couple organizing a trip. While one partner longs for an exciting mountain hike, the other fantasizes about a tranquil beach vacation. This preference disparity could become a tiresome deadlock if no compromise is made. However, if they are willing to make concessions, they may find a seaside town with hiking trails nearby, satisfying their needs for adventure and leisure.

Compromise requires a careful balancing act between collaboration and assertiveness. It's about considering your partner's viewpoint while simultaneously advocating your demands. Finding a solution that respects each person and improves the relationship is more important than winning and losing.

Knowing your wants and priorities is often the first step in this approach. In this case, what is the most important thing to you? Where are you flexible, and what are your non-negotiables? After you have a solid understanding of your desires, you may successfully express them to your spouse.

For instance, the beach-loving partner may realize that their primary desire in the vacation setting is to unwind and escape the stress of everyday life. As long as there are chances for relaxation and renewal, they might not be picky about the exact place. Their adventure-seeking companion may acknowledge their need for exploration and physical exercise. As long as there is some degree of difficulty and excitement, they may be receptive to many adventures.

The pair can negotiate cooperatively if they understand their respective requirements well. This calls for candid dialogue, attentive listening, and an openness to coming up with original answers. They may look at alternate holiday spots that combine beaches and mountains, investigate alternate activities that cater to their interests, or even consider dividing their time between two distinct places.

The secret to a successful negotiation is to identify points of agreement. What goals or values do you both have in common? Both parties may prioritize making enduring memories and spending quality time together throughout the vacation. Finding a compromise that meets their unique needs and fortifies their relationship might be based on this shared value.

Meeting precisely in the middle is not usually the definition of compromise. One partner may concede on one subject in return for the other partner conceding another. It could entail coming up with an original solution that meets the needs of both partners in a way neither had initially thought possible.

For instance, if the adventure-seeking partner agrees to spend a few days lounging by a lake or getting spa treatments, the beach-loving partner might consent to a mountain getaway. Alternatively, they may find a place that provides access to the beach and chances for outdoor pursuits like biking, hiking, etc.

Compromise demands adaptability and a readiness to explore different options. It's about realizing that there may be more than one way to solve the problem and that an alternative strategy might better meet your needs.

The following techniques will help you become an expert in negotiating and reaching compromises:

1. Active Listening: Take note of your partner's body language, tone of voice, and words. Repeat what you have heard to ensure you comprehend their point of view. Inquire further to gain a deeper understanding.

2. Empathy: Try to understand your partner's perspective by placing yourself in their shoes. If you disagree with their viewpoint, respect their emotions and affirm their experience.

3. Assertiveness: Confidently communicate your demands and wants. Use "I" statements to express your sentiments without blaming or criticizing your partner.

4. Brainstorming: Without passing judgment, come up with a range of potential answers. Promote originality and look into possibilities you may not have initially thought of.

5. Flexibility: You must be able to modify your expectations and consider other options. Understand that reaching a compromise frequently entails identifying a middle ground that meets both parties' needs.

6. Concentrate on Common Objectives: Remember your common principles and objectives. This can help you maintain your focus on identifying a solution that is advantageous to the partnership overall.

7. Take Breaks: If the discussion gets heated or fruitless, take a moment to collect yourself and gather perspective. When you are more willing to make concessions, bring up the topic again.

8. Celebrate Your Successes: After you reach an agreement, pat yourself on the back. This promotes future compromise and highlights the benefits of teamwork.

Gaining proficiency in bargaining and compromise is a continuous process that strengthens with repetition. You may change disputes from a battlefield into a chance for development, closeness, and a stronger bond by approaching arguments with an open mind, an open mind, and a desire to listen, comprehend, and find common ground.

Moving from Win-Lose to Win-Win Solutions

Consider resolving conflicts as a game. In a win-lose situation, one player wins, and the other loses. This strategy might be effective in competitive sports, but it sows discord, resentment, and the seeds of future disputes in interpersonal relationships. We must change our perspective from one of competition to one of cooperation, looking for win-win solutions that are advantageous to both parties to foster a solid and successful partnership.

This change necessitates a fundamental adjustment in viewpoint. Reframe conflict as a puzzle that needs to be solved collectively rather than as a fight to be won. Instead of being argumentative, approach arguments with curiosity, trying to understand your partner's point of view rather than just stating your own.

Consider a couple that can't agree on how to spend their tax return. While one partner envisions a lavish vacation, the other wants to use the funds for a much-needed home makeover. In a win-lose situation, one spouse may push the other aside and insist on their preferred course of action, making the other feel ignored and angry.

Both spouses politely and freely communicate their wishes in a win-win situation. While the travel-loving partner may express their desire for adventure and getaway, the renovation-minded mate may discuss their worries about the old kitchen and leaky roof. By hearing each other's viewpoints, they may find a solution that works for both, such as a more modest refurbishment that frees up funds for a quicker, less expensive trip.

This cooperative method necessitates a readiness to make concessions, consider other options, and devise innovative solutions that satisfy the needs of both parties. It's about realizing that there may be other options besides your original concept and that a different strategy might result in a more satisfying outcome for you both.

The following guidelines can help you find win-win solutions:

1. Disentangle the Individual from the Issue: Instead of criticizing your partner's character, concentrate on the current problem. Instead of placing blame or offering criticism, positively voice your concerns. Rather than stating, "You're always so irresponsible with money," try expressing, "I'm concerned about our spending habits and how they might affect our financial goals." Can we talk about this together?

2. Find Common Interests: Seek out areas of agreement and similar objectives. What are you both hoping to accomplish? Which values are similar among you? Concentrating on common interests might facilitate finding solutions that work for both couples. For example, if spouses value experiences and financial stability, they can balance taking infrequent holidays or splurges and saving for the future.

3. Create a Range of Options: Before making a choice, consider a number of potential options. Promote originality and consider options you may not have considered first. This broadens the scope and raises the possibility of a solution that benefits everyone.

4. Apply Objective Criteria: Objective criteria help you decide when weighing your options. This could entail considering elements like price, time commitment, or possible effects on other facets of your life. For instance, the couple may weigh the costs, time commitments, and potential effects on their long-term financial objectives while choosing between a vacation and home improvement.

5. Communicate Clearly and Respectfully: Use "I" statements and refrain from using accusatory language when expressing your wants and concerns. Recognize your partner's feelings and carefully listen to their point of view. This establishes a secure environment for candid dialogue and group problem-solving.

6. Be Willing to Compromise: Understand that reaching a compromise is necessary to arrive at win-win solutions. Be adaptable and prepared to lower your standards. Think about your non-negotiables and what you're willing to give up. This enables you to reach a compromise that meets the needs of both parties.

7. Celebrate Your Successes: When you come up with a solution that benefits everyone, take pride in your accomplishment. This promotes future compromise and highlights the benefits of teamwork. Additionally, it reminds you that you are on the same team and enhances your relationship.

It takes a mental change and a dedication to teamwork to move from win-lose to win-win solutions. By addressing conflict with a cooperative, empathetic, and innovative attitude to problem-solving, you can turn arguments from battlefields into chances for development, connection, and a more solid, satisfying partnership.

Setting Healthy Boundaries and Respecting Differences

Consider your partnership as a communal garden. Each partner contributes unique flowers, herbs, and veggies to create a lively and blooming atmosphere. However, limits are necessary even in the most harmonious garden. Without distinct boundaries, invading weeds could choke out fragile blossoms, or one plant could overgrow and suffocate another.

Establishing sound boundaries in relationships is similar to caring for this garden, ensuring every plant has the room and materials it needs to flourish. Even in the face of conflict, it's about stating your needs, setting clear boundaries, and honoring your partner's uniqueness. Boundaries are fences that safeguard and maintain each person's individual beauty in the relationship, not walls that split.

Consider a pair whose social demands are varied. While one partner enjoys peaceful evenings at home, the other thrives on many social events and excursions. When there are unclear limits, one partner may feel pressured to attend events they don't like, while the other feels ignored and undervalued, which could lead to resentment.

Establishing healthy boundaries may entail being open and honest about each partner's wants and requirements in this situation. To give the homebody more time to enjoy solitude, the social butterfly may agree to restrict their outings to specific days of the week. As a sign of support for their partner's needs, the homebody may occasionally consent to social gatherings.

Boundaries cover many relationship elements, from physical contact and personal space to emotional needs and time obligations. By defining what each person finds acceptable and comfortable, they establish a sense of safety and respect in the partnership.

Understanding that boundaries may differ from your partner's is an essential part of defining boundaries. What one person finds pleasant may be invasive or constrictive to another. Keeping a healthy and balanced relationship requires respecting these variances.

For instance, one spouse may require a lot of physical touch, while the other may need more privacy. To respect these differences, finding a solution that meets the requirements of both partners, like planning regular cuddling time while allowing for times of autonomous activities, may be necessary.

It's crucial to express your boundaries in a solid and unambiguous manner. Don't give away too much or assume your partner can read your thoughts. Instead, politely and directly communicate your needs. To express your boundaries without placing blame or criticizing your partner, use "I" phrases. Instead of stating, "You always interrupt me when I'm talking," for example, try saying, "I feel unheard when I'm interrupted." Please hold off on sharing your opinions until I've finished speaking.

Another aspect of setting limits is saying "no" when required. This can be difficult, particularly for people-pleasers or conflict-averse people. However, saying "no" to demands or actions that cross your boundaries is self-respecting and emotionally healthy.

Respect your partner's needs and listen to them with empathy when they set boundaries. Do not minimize their emotions or attempt to persuade them to reconsider. Instead, respect their boundaries and collaborate to discover solutions that meet their demands while respecting your own.

Respecting diversity transcends national borders. It's about respecting your partner's distinct character, beliefs, and passions, even if they diverge from yours. It's about realizing that these distinctions add to your relationship's depth and complexity.

It's easy to get caught up in the details of a dispute and lose sight of the wider picture. Remind yourself of your shared values, the traits you admire in your partner, and the things that bring you together. This change in viewpoint might promote an appreciation for your partner's uniqueness and defuse tension.

Avoiding attempts to alter your spouse is another aspect of respecting diversity. Building a happy and successful relationship requires accepting them for who they are, flaws and all. This means valuing your partner's fundamental qualities, but it does not imply that you cannot support one another's personal development or foster growth.

As your partnership develops, respecting differences and establishing appropriate limits are lifelong habits that call for constant discussion, compromise, and flexibility.

Key Points

- Compromise is about finding solutions that satisfy your partner's and your own needs; it is not about one person succeeding or failing.

- Before engaging in a negotiation, clearly define your personal needs and priorities. Be aware of the things you can and cannot compromise on.

- Finding common ground and comprehending your partner's viewpoint need active listening and empathy.

- Brainstorming a range of alternatives, including original ideas you might not have considered, can produce more fulfilling results.

- Celebrate successful compromises to promote the positive features of teamwork and encourage further cooperation.

Self-Reflection Questions

1. Are you ever inclined to concentrate more on achieving your goals or coming up with a compromise that benefits you and your partner during arguments?

_____

_____

_____

_____

_____

2. How adept are you at determining your objectives and requirements before negotiating? Do you take the time to identify your priorities?

_____

_____

_____

_____

_____

3. How well do you hear what your partner says when you disagree? Do you make an effort to comprehend their requirements and worries?

_____

_____

_____
_____
_____

4. How adaptable are you to considering other options? Do you stick with your original concept or consider other possibilities?

_____
_____
_____
_____
_____

5. When you have to compromise, how do you usually respond? Do you see it as a setback or as a necessary step toward a win-win situation?

_____
_____
_____
_____
_____

Chapter 9: Reframing Conflict as an Opportunity

"The obstacle is the path." - Zen Proverb

This ancient insight represents a significant paradigm shift: problems, rather than impediments to progress, become the very terrain on which we grow and adapt. Conflict, commonly viewed as a danger to peace in relationships, can also catalyze deeper connection, understanding, and intimacy. Reframing conflict as an opportunity necessitates a mental shift, a willingness to see differences not as battles to be won or lost but as opportunities to learn, grow, and deepen the links that bind us.

Consider a couple of bickering over home tasks. One partner is overwhelmed by their obligations, while the other feels underappreciated for their efforts. Instead of interpreting this dispute as a sign of incompatibility or hate, they can reframe it as an opportunity to explain their needs, renegotiate their roles, and build a more fair and happy relationship.

This shift in viewpoint begins with acknowledging that conflict is an unavoidable aspect of any relationship. No two people have the same values, priorities, and interests. Disagreements are inevitable as you navigate the complexity of life together. Rather than fearing or avoiding conflict, accept it as a natural and beneficial component of a healthy partnership.

Conflict, when treated constructively, can be a tremendous chance for growth. It allows you to understand your partner's needs, values, and opinions. It challenges you to question your preconceptions and biases, broadening your awareness of yourself and the world around you. It challenges you to improve your communication and problem-solving abilities, resulting in a more robust and flexible partnership.

Unmet needs are frequently the root cause of disagreement. One partner may want more quality time, while the other demands more liberty. One person may value spontaneity, while the other prefers routine and predictability. Conflict can bring these demands to the surface, allowing you to address them openly and develop solutions that satisfy both partners' goals.

For example, a spouse who values quality time may desire more shared experiences and a committed connection. The partner who values autonomy may express a need for personal space and time to pursue individual interests. By recognizing and validating one another's needs, they can build a more fulfilling and balanced connection.

Conflict can also highlight places where your beliefs and expectations disagree. One couple prioritizes financial security and long-term savings, whereas the other loves experiences and enjoys spending on travel and leisure. If not addressed, these differences can result in recurrent confrontations and animosity.

However, viewing this conflict as an opportunity, the couple can discuss their financial principles and ambitions. They may discover common objectives and goals or unearth deeper financial concerns and anxieties. Open communication can result in a better knowledge of one another and a more collaborative approach to economic decision-making.

Conflict can also be a catalyst for personal development. It requires assessing your communication patterns, conflict resolution techniques, and emotional triggers. It encourages you to become more self-aware, empathetic, and compassionate.

For example, conflict can reveal this pattern and encourage you to develop more vital coping skills if you are prone to getting defensive during disagreements. You can pause before reacting, actively listen to your partner's point of view, or assertively voice your requirements.

A mentality shift is required to reframe conflict as an opportunity. Instead of seeing arguments as dangers to your relationship, consider them opportunities to enhance your bond, improve your understanding, and create a more rewarding partnership.

Here are some strategies to help you reframe the conflict.

1. Focus on the Positive: Consider the potential positives rather than obsessing about the negative parts of disagreement. What can you glean from

this disagreement? How will this challenge improve your relationship?

2. Practice Gratitude: Express gratitude to your spouse for the opportunity to work through issues together. This can help you shift your focus from negativity to thankfulness.

3. Seek Understanding: Approach conflict with curiosity, not judgment. Even if you disagree with your partner, try to comprehend their point of view.

4. Take Responsibility: Accept your personal role in the disagreement, take responsibility for your actions, and apologize for any harm you may have caused.

5. Focus on Solutions: Instead of concentrating on the problem, find solutions that work for both of you. Consider your options, reach concessions, and celebrate your triumphs.

6. Practice Forgiveness: Forgive yourself and your partner for mistakes or unpleasant remarks. Forgiveness allows you to let go of hate and start fresh.

7. View disagreement as a Growth Opportunity: See disagreement as an opportunity to learn, grow, and strengthen your relationship. Accept the challenge and believe you will emerge more robust and united from the disagreement.

Reframing disagreement as an opportunity is an excellent technique for transforming your relationship. By changing your perspective and seeing arguments as opportunities for growth and connection, you may build a more resilient, rewarding, and loving partnership.

Shifting Perspectives: Seeing the Positive in Disagreements

Imagine a winding mountain road. The climb appears frightening from the bottom, with bends and sharp inclines. However, fresh views emerge as you ascend, showing spectacular panoramas and secret valleys. Similarly, relationship disagreement, generally viewed as a challenging climb, can expose hidden strengths and improve your bond.

Shifting your viewpoint on conflict requires a deliberate effort to see past the present frustration and discomfort. It's about accepting that arguments while challenging, maybe catalysts for growth, understanding, and a deeper connection with your relationship.

Think of conflict as a mirror, reflecting elements of yourself and your relationship that might go unnoticed. Disagreements can reveal unmet needs, unspoken emotions, and opposing values. Instead of avoiding this reflection, see it as an opportunity for self-discovery and deeper intimacy.

For example, a frequent fight about punctuality may indicate one partner's deep-seated fear of wasting time. In contrast, the other partner may understand they use tardiness to establish control or express a subconscious revolt against the structure. Recognizing these underlying concerns allows the couple to address the leading cause of the disagreement rather than simply arguing over surface-level conduct.

Another method to change your perspective is to see conflict as a crucible for resilience. Just like a blacksmith forges steel in the high heat of a fire, partnerships improve as they navigate problems together. When treated constructively, each conflict provides an opportunity to develop essential skills such as communication, compromise, and empathy.

Instead of perceiving disagreement as a sign of weakness or incompatibility, consider it an opportunity to build a stronger and more resilient partnership. Each time you successfully resolve a conflict, you deepen your bond, instilling greater trust and confidence in your capacity to weather future storms.

Conflict can also be a catalyst for personal development. It asks you to explore your communication patterns, emotional triggers, and conflict resolution techniques. It encourages you to become more self-aware, empathetic, and compassionate.

For example, if you tend to shut down or retreat during arguments, conflict might reveal this habit and inspire you to develop stronger coping skills. You may learn to voice your wants more assertively, actively listen to your partner's point of view, or better manage your emotions.

Shifting your viewpoint on conflict involves deliberately questioning your assumptions and rethinking your thinking. Here are some activities that will help you identify the positive possibilities in arguments.

1. The Gratitude Lens: After a conflict, reflect on what you learned from the event. Did you better grasp your partner's needs and perspectives? Did you discover anything new about yourself? Express gratitude for the opportunity to develop and strengthen your friendship.

2. The "What If" Game: To challenge your negative ideas about conflict, use "what if" questions. Instead of thinking, "This argument means we're incompatible," consider, "What if this disagreement helps us clarify our needs and build a stronger foundation for our relationship?"

3. Empathy Exercise: Put yourself in your partner's shoes and try to understand the problem from their point of view. What are they feeling or experiencing? What needs or fears may be influencing their behavior? This activity can increase empathy and compassion while decreasing defensiveness and boosting understanding.

4. The Reframing Challenge: Recognize a recurring dispute in your relationship and view it as a chance for improvement. For example, if you frequently disagree about finances, reframe the argument as an opportunity to develop a shared financial vision and work toward a more secure future together.

5. The Conflict Resolution notebook: Keep a notebook dedicated to monitoring your conflicts and reflecting on the lessons learned. Document the trigger, the emotions involved, the communication methods, and the result of the conflict. Use this notebook to detect recurring patterns, measure your progress toward conflict resolution skills, and celebrate your accomplishments.

Shifting your viewpoint on conflict is a practical approach that can alter your relationship.

Using Conflict to Deepen Intimacy and Understanding

Consider a pearl. It starts as a little irritant, like a grain of sand stuck in the shell of an oyster. However, the oyster turns this annoyance into something lovely and priceless via layers of tenderness and grit. Similarly, although it can be awkward and difficult, conflict in a relationship can spur development, closeness, and a better understanding of one another.

When handled well, conflict presents a unique chance to unveil your true selves and peel aside the layers of regular interactions. It's an opportunity to go beyond superficial discussions and investigate the fundamental ideals, convictions, and aspirations that influence your unique experiences.

Imagine a couple who can't agree on what to do on the weekends. While one partner enjoys a calm routine at home, the other yearns for unpredictability and excitement. They can utilize this difference as a starting point for more in-depth discussion rather than letting it cause them to grow apart. While the homebody may express a need for relaxation and renewal, the adventurous partner may share their desire for novelty and excitement. A more satisfying compromise and a deeper understanding of one another's viewpoints can result from this candid discussion of needs and wants.

Vulnerabilities can also be revealed by conflict. During a heated argument, you may reveal vulnerabilities or concerns you usually keep to yourself. This openness can feel dangerous but also fosters a deep sense of intimacy. You develop trust and strengthen your relationship by letting your spouse see you for who you are, flaws, and all.

Consider a dispute between a couple over alleged inattention. The other partner is accused by one of being emotionally unavailable and aloof. Rather than reacting defensively, the accused partner may openly discuss their difficulties, showing affection or fear of closeness. Because of this openness, a bridge of understanding may be built, enabling the other partner to provide support and empathy instead of condemnation.

Conflict can reveal the outlines of your partner's inner life when handled well. It offers insight into their goals, values, and aspirations. By carefully listening to them and trying to grasp their point of view, you can better comprehend them and their priorities.

For instance, a quarrel regarding a career move may indicate that one partner wants their employment to have more meaning and fulfillment. Alternatively, a disagreement over a social obligation may reveal a yearning for a closer bond with friends or a fear of missing out. These conflict-based insights can deepen your relationship and help you understand your mate better.

Additionally, conflict can point out areas for personal and marital development. A financial dispute exposes a history of rash purchases or worrying about running out of money. A disagreement about housework highlights the need for more cooperation and communication. By recognizing these trends and resolving the underlying problems, you can utilize disagreement as a launching pad for relationship and personal growth.

Constructive conflict resolution frequently makes couples feel more devoted to and appreciative of one another after arguments. They get better at communicating, navigating differences, and encouraging one another's development. They gain resilience that enables them to face challenges in the future with more poise and assurance.

Here are a few instances of how couples might utilize disagreement to deepen their relationship:

- When a couple disagrees about parenting styles, they look into alternative methods and go to a parenting class together, which helps them develop a more cooperative and consistent parenting style.

- A couple's financial goals become more transparent and aligned when they develop a common financial vision and budget after a disagreement over a significant purchase.

- A disagreement about insufficient quality time inspires a couple to plan frequent date nights and give priority to activities they both enjoy, strengthening their bond and rekindling their romance.

- A couple gains better knowledge and respect for one another's preferences when they openly discuss their unique requirements for social contact and alone time after a disagreement over a social obligation.

- Following a furious dispute, a couple takes some time to cool down before continuing the conversation, emphasizing hearing each other out, showing gratitude, and restating their devotion to one another.

Despite being frequently uncomfortable, conflict can lead to significant development and connection. By addressing conflicts with curiosity, vulnerability, and a dedication to understanding, you can increase intimacy, fortify your relationship, and build a more robust and satisfying partnership.

Key Points

- Any relationship will inevitably experience conflict, but when managed well, it can present opportunities for development and a closer bond.

- Unmet needs are frequently the root cause of disagreements; conflict can highlight these needs and provide an opportunity to address them directly.

- Conflict can reveal disparities in expectations and ideals, leading to insightful discussions and a better understanding of one another.

- Analyze your communication techniques, conflict resolution methods, and emotional triggers to use conflict as a springboard for personal development.

- Reframe disagreement as an opportunity to improve your relationship, broaden your understanding, and forge a more satisfying alliance.

Self-Reflection Questions

1. Do you see a dispute in your relationship as an opportunity or a threat?

_____
_____
_____
_____
_____

2. How do you usually handle conflict? Do you try to comprehend your partner's point of view, shut down, or get defensive?

_____
_____
_____
_____
_____

3. Do you see any recurring issues in your partnership? Which unfulfilled wants or conflicting values could be causing these trends?

_____
_____

_____

_____

_____

4. What have previous arguments taught you and your partner about each other?

_____

_____

_____

_____

5. How can you turn upcoming arguments into chances to improve your relationship and enhance your bonds?

_____

_____

_____

_____

_____

Part 4
<u>Sustaining Connection in the Long Term</u>

Chapter 10: When Conflict Becomes Unhealthy

"Love is not a feeling; it's an action." - Dr. Steve Maraboli

Maraboli's comments draw attention to an important distinction: love is not only a passive feeling; instead, it is an active decision and a verb that calls for work, dedication, and a readiness to support your partner, particularly in trying times. Any partnership will inevitably experience conflict, but healthy disputes and toxic habits of abuse and control are very different. Making wise decisions regarding your relationship and safeguarding your well-being depend on your ability to spot the warning signals of unhealthy conflict.

Imagine a couple fighting. One spouse speaks louder, expressing disdain and condemnation in their remarks. The other partner withdraws with their shoulders hunched and their words hardly audible above a whisper. A potentially harmful dynamic is indicated by this power imbalance, in which one spouse continuously exercises control while the other feels silenced and devalued.

Unhealthy conflict frequently forms a pattern of recurring actions meant to degrade, control, or manipulate a partner. These actions can be overt or covert, ranging from overt violence and aggressiveness to covert putdowns and guilt trips.

The frequent use of personal insults is a classic indicator of unhealthy conflict. Name-calling, insults, or character assassinations may be used by the abusive partner in place of addressing a particular behavior or problem. To undermine their partner's self-esteem and keep power, they may be critical of their personality, IQ, or looks.

The use of threats or intimidation is another warning sign. This could be shouting, hurling things, slamming doors, or making threatening motions. To instill fear and control, the abusive partner may threaten to hurt their partner, their loved ones, or even themselves.

Another strategy frequently used in toxic partnerships is isolation. The violent spouse may attempt to restrict their partner's interactions with friends and family, keep tabs on their texts and phone conversations, or regulate their social media presence. The victim becomes dependent as a result of this isolation and finds it more challenging to ask for assistance or support.

Abuse might also take the form of financial control. The abusive partner may limit their partner's economic resources, manage their expenditures, or keep them from seeking employment or education. The victim may find it difficult to exit the relationship due to this financial dependence.

Although the wounds from emotional abuse may not be as apparent, they can nonetheless be just as harmful as those from physical assault. Gaslighting, a manipulative technique that involves warping reality and making the victim question their senses and sanity, may be employed by the abusive partner. To make the victim feel confused and uneasy, they may twist their words, deny past events, or make unfounded charges.

An abusive and apologetic cycle is a common feature of unhealthy conflict. In between outbursts of anger and repentance, the abusive partner may lavish their partner with presents, apologies, or promises of reform. The victim may find it challenging to end the relationship because of the perplexing and addictive dynamic this cycle can produce.

Understanding the warning signals of unhealthy conflict is essential to safeguarding your well-being. If you feel threatened, manipulated, or denigrated in your relationship regularly, it's critical to get support and assistance. Consult a domestic violence helpline, therapist, family member, or trusted friend. These sites can offer direction, encouragement, and tools to help you make wise decisions regarding your future and safety.

Remember that you are entitled to decency and respect. Regardless of your relationship status, no one has the right to manipulate or mistreat you. Seek assistance if you're going through an unhealthy conflict. You're not by yourself.

The following resources may be helpful:

- 1-800-799-7233 is the National Domestic Violence Hotline number.
- 1-800-656-HOPE is the National Sexual Assault Hotline.

- nnedv.org is the website of the National Network to End Domestic Violence.
- ncadv.org, the National Coalition Against Domestic Violence

These organizations provide resources, information, and confidential support to assist you in navigating harmful relationships and building a secure and satisfying future.

Recognizing the Signs of Emotional Abuse

Emotional abuse damages the spirit, destroying self-worth and warping reality, whereas physical violence produces outwardly noticeable scars. It's a subtle kind of control that frequently goes unnoticed, leaving victims feeling bewildered, alone, and questioning their sanity. Making wise decisions regarding your relationship and safeguarding your well-being depend on your ability to spot the warning signs of emotional abuse.

A series of actions intended to manipulate, control, or degrade a relationship is known as emotional abuse. A person's emotional and psychological health is attacked, resulting in a sense of helplessness and reliance as well as a decline in self-esteem. These actions can be overt or covert, frequently passed off as "jokes" or "concerns," making them hard to spot.

Embarrassment is a popular emotional abuse method. The abuser may say disparaging things about their partner's accomplishments, IQ, or looks. They could minimize their partner's thoughts or reject their emotions, making them feel inadequate and unworthy. This may sound like, "You're so stupid, you can't even do that right," or "You're lucky anyone even wants to be with you."

Another fundamental component of emotional abuse is control. The abuser may try to control their partner's decisions about everything from their spending patterns and professional goals to their attire and social circles. They may monitor their partner's calls and messages, keep tabs on their social media activities, or cut them off from family and friends. This control makes the sufferer feel helpless and trapped in a suffocating environment.

A particularly pernicious kind of emotional abuse is gaslighting, which entails warping reality and causing the victim to question their sense of reality and sanity. To make the victim feel confused and insecure, the abuser may twist their words, make unfounded allegations, or deny past events. This may come out as "You're making that up." That never happened," or "If you believe that's what I meant, you're insane."

Threats and intimidation frequently accompany emotional abuse. The abuser may smash doors, hurl objects, yell, or make threatening motions. They may incite fear and control by threatening to hurt themselves, their loved ones, or their partner.

Blaming and accusing the victim of the abuser's actions is another form of emotional abuse. "You made me do this" or "I wouldn't have gotten angry if you hadn't said that" are examples of statements the abuser may make. This strategy places the blame on the victim, giving them the impression that they are to blame for the abuse.

Emotional manipulation can sometimes take the shape of silent treatment or withholding affection.

As a form of control or punishment, the abuser may refrain from intimacy, communication, or displays of love. The victim becomes dependent and insecure as a result, feeling worried and needy for their partner's acceptance.

It might be challenging to spot the warning signs of emotional abuse, particularly when it's disguised as sincere love and concern. A perplexing and addictive loop may result from the abuser alternating between loving conduct and violent outbursts. The victim may minimize the harm to their well-being, justify their partner's actions, or hold themselves responsible for the abuse.

Seeking Help: Therapy and Other Resources

Seeking help is frequently seen as an admission of failure and an indication that we cannot solve our difficulties. Nonetheless, asking for help shows bravery, self-awareness, and a dedication to development. Seeking assistance can be the lifeline that saves you from the verge of disconnection in intimate relationships and puts you on the road to recovery and closer ties.

Imagine a couple stuck in a pattern of arguing all the time. Their emotional scars are festering, their communication patterns are ingrained, and they feel trapped. Despite their love for one another, they are unsure of how to overcome the damaging habits that could weaken their relationship. Getting professional assistance—whether in the form of individual counseling or couples therapy—can offer the direction and encouragement needed to overcome these obstacles and build a more satisfying relationship.

Therapy provides a private, secure setting for discussing your communication preferences, interpersonal patterns, and personal requirements. A competent therapist serves as a mentor, encouraging dialogue, providing resources and techniques for resolving disputes, and assisting you in gaining a better knowledge of one another and yourself.

You can benefit from couple's therapy:

- Determine and resolve underlying issues: Deeper-seated problems, such as unresolved past hurts, conflicting values, or unfulfilled needs, frequently cause recurring confrontations. A therapist can assist you in identifying these underlying problems and creating positive coping mechanisms.

- Develop your communication skills because misunderstandings can lead to conflict. A therapist can teach you more effective communication techniques, including assertive expression, active listening, and conflict resolution.

- Develop closeness and intimacy: Lack of intimacy and emotional distance can lead to conflict. With the support of a therapist, you may strengthen your relationship, promote emotional safety, and reestablish connection.

- Create more constructive conflict resolution techniques: Although disagreements will inevitably arise in any relationship, how you respond to them will determine its success. A therapist can assist you in overcoming harmful habits and creating more constructive conflict-resolution techniques.

With therapy's support, you can rekindle the spark of connection, uncover your relationship's strengths, and create a more robust and satisfying partnership.

A successful therapeutic experience depends on selecting the appropriate therapist. Look for a therapist with experience dealing with the particular issues you're encountering and specializing in couples counseling. Referrals from friends, relatives, or your physician can help you locate a therapist. You can also look through online directories such as Psychology Today or GoodTherapy.

When selecting a therapist, take into account the following:

- Experience and qualifications: Verify if they possess the necessary certifications and licenses to practice treatment.

- Therapeutic approach: Different therapists use different methods. Look into other methods, such as the Gottman Method, emotionally focused therapy (EFT), or cognitive behavioral therapy (CBT), and select a therapist whose style suits your requirements and preferences.

- Personality and style: Trust and connection are essential for a successful therapeutic alliance. Select a therapist who makes you feel at ease and understood.

Numerous different services can provide support and direction for your relationship in addition to treatment. These consist of:

Workshops and retreats on relationships provide:

- A controlled setting for picking up new skills.
- Networking with other couples.
- Getting advice from relationship specialists.

Self-help books and articles: Many books and articles provide helpful advice and resources for enhancing communication, handling conflict, and fortifying your bond.

Support groups: Making connections with other couples experiencing comparable difficulties can help foster a feeling of camaraderie, understanding, and support.

Online resources: Websites and applications offer many exercises, tools, and knowledge to help you improve your relationship.

Asking for assistance shows that you are dedicated to your relationship and prepared to invest in its development, not that you are weak. By asking for help, you can access essential resources and direction to overcome obstacles, deepen your relationship, and build a more resilient and satisfying partnership.

Key Points

- While unhealthy conflict involves abuse, manipulation, or control habits, healthy conflict involves disagreements and divergent viewpoints.

- Financial control, isolation, intimidation, and personal attacks are all warning signs of possible abuse.

- Deep emotional scars can result from emotional abuse, including gaslighting, which can be equally as harmful as physical violence.

- It can be challenging to end a relationship that involves cycles of violence and apologies because they can produce a perplexing and manipulative dynamic.

- It's critical to identify the warning signs of unhealthy conflict to safeguard one's well-being and seek assistance when necessary.

Self-Reflection Questions

1. Do you dread your partner's reaction when disagreeing with them, or do you feel comfortable voicing your opinions?

_____

_____

_____

_____

2. When you argue, does your partner ever use put downs, name-calling, or insults?

_____

_____

_____

_____

3. Has your spouse tried to limit your social interactions or distance you from friends or family?

_____

_____

_____

_____

_____

4. Do you believe you and your partner have equal financial control, or does your partner restrict your financial resources?

_____

_____

_____

_____

5. Does your partner ever cause you to question your senses or sanity, or do they ever make you question your memory by denying past events?

_____

_____

_____

_____

Chapter 11: Cultivating a Culture of Love and Respect

"Love does not dominate; it cultivates." - Johann Wolfgang von Goethe

The essence of a loving relationship is encapsulated in Goethe's words: a partnership in which both parties feel respected, cared for, and empowered to develop. More than simply avoiding conflict is necessary to foster such a relationship; it also calls for a deliberate attempt to establish a culture of love and respect, a rich environment where bonds are strengthened, and arguments are used as stepping stones to greater understanding.

Imagine a garden. With their tastes in flowers, herbs, and vegetables, two gardeners care for their separate plots. They celebrate one another's harvests, exchange tools, and give each other guidance. Sometimes, their tastes diverge—one likes a wildflower meadow, the other a neat rose garden. Nevertheless, they treat these distinctions with deference, figuring out how to respect one another's preferences and produce a harmonious landscape.

This garden metaphor exemplifies the core of fostering a culture of love and respect in a partnership. It involves valuing and respecting one another's uniqueness, being honest and open in communication, and fostering the bond that unites you.

Appreciation is a vital component of our culture. No matter how tiny, expressing thanks for your partner's presence creates a pleasant and affirming environment. Please take note of their small actions, such as their ability to make you laugh, their considerate gifts, and the work they put into their relationship. Express your gratitude by saying something like, "I love how you always make me feel heard," or "I appreciate you taking care of the dishes tonight."

Little deeds of kindness have a significant impact.

After a long day:
- Give your partner a back rub.

- Put a heartfelt message on the bathroom mirror.
- Surprise them with their favorite cuisine.

These actions show that you are thoughtful and kind, which improves your relationship and fosters feelings of warmth and love.

The cornerstone of a strong relationship is respect. It's about respecting your partner's limits, values, and opinions—even if they don't align with yours. It's about being considerate and courteous to people, even when disagreeing. Steer clear of insults, name-calling, and verbal or emotional abuse. These actions undermine confidence and foster an atmosphere of anxiety and unease.

Respect also entails respecting your partner's independence. Acknowledge that they are unique people with needs, wants, and views of their own. Refrain from attempting to influence or alter them. Instead, please encourage them to follow their passions and aspirations while supporting their growth.

Honest and open communication is essential to fostering a culture of respect and love. Talk to your spouse about your needs, wants, and feelings, and urge them to do the same. Even if you disagree with their viewpoint, actively listen to it. Acknowledge their experience and validate their feelings.

When disagreements occur, handle them with a collaborative rather than competitive mindset. Make an effort to comprehend your partner's perspective while politely and clearly communicating your own requirements. Instead of attempting to "win" the disagreement, concentrate on finding solutions that benefit you both.

Establishing connection rituals can improve your relationship and foster a feeling of purpose. Depending on your tastes, these rituals can be as straightforward or complex as you choose. They could include a weekly ritual of preparing a special meal together, a daily practice of expressing thankfulness, or a monthly date night where you try something new or visit a different area of your city.

These routines give your partnership a feeling of stability and regularity in the midst of life's storms. They also remind you of the love and gratitude that unite you by fostering chances for connection, laughing and shared joy.

Nurturing Appreciation and Gratitude

Fostering thankfulness and appreciation in your relationship builds a strong foundation for connection, fortifies your relationship, and acts as a buffer against the unavoidable storms of conflict.

Imagine a couple getting ready for the day. A modest gesture of service that makes a big impression is when one partner makes coffee the way the other likes. The other partner shows their appreciation by grinning broadly and saying, "Thank you." This brief conversation establishes a good tone for the day, strengthening their bond and reminding them of their shared concern and consideration for one another.

It's easy to take our relationships for granted in the daily grind. We frequently forget the little deeds of kindness and the innumerable ways they improve our lives because we grow accustomed to their love, support, and presence. Developing gratitude requires a deliberate change in viewpoint and a readiness to observe and value the commonplace but frequently overlooked moments.

Start by focusing on the little things. Please note how your partner makes an effort to prepare a meal, how they welcome you in the morning, or how they pay close attention when you express your feelings and opinions. These seemingly unimportant deeds frequently reveal much about their devotion and love.

Verbally, thank them. Express to your partner how much you appreciate having them in your life. Thank them for their contributions to the partnership, and acknowledge their efforts. A simple "thank you" can make a big difference in fostering an appreciative society.

Express your gratitude for your relationship in a meaningful letter or message. Explain the traits you find admirable, how they make you feel loved, and how they affect your life. Your partner can treasure this material token of your gratitude and look at it whenever they need a reminder of your affection.

Small deeds of compassion can also express gratitude. After a long day:

- Give your partner a back rub.
- Put a heartfelt message on the bathroom mirror.
- Surprise them with their favorite cuisine.

These actions show that you are thoughtful and kind, which improves your relationship and fosters feelings of warmth and love.

A general gratitude attitude for your partner's existence in your life is just as important as expressing appreciation for their deeds. Every day, consider the traits you value in your spouse, the happiness they provide, and the ways they improve your life. This technique can help you change your viewpoint from negativity to gratitude, which will result in a more satisfying and happy relationship.

Gratitude can help prevent conflict. Recalling the reasons, you value your partner during arguments might help reduce tension and prevent it from getting worse. It might serve as a reminder of the greater good, the love and dedication that unite you despite disagreements.

For instance, you could take a moment during a furious dispute to remind yourself of your partner's generosity, sense of humor, or steadfast support. This change of emphasis can help you become more empathetic and less angry and open the door to a more productive dialogue.

Recognizing the importance of your partner in your life, showing your gratitude in words and deeds, and developing an overall thankful mindset are all parts of nurturing appreciation and gratitude.

Creating Rituals for Connection and Intimacy

Consider your partnership as a building you construct together, one brick at a time. Rituals are the solid framework that offers stability and strength, the mortar that keeps those bricks together. They are the recurrent themes, the well-known beats that break up your days and weeks, providing stability and shared purpose in life's uncertain course.

Imagine that a couple shares three things they value about one another and their life as part of their "gratitude practice," which they do after each day. Repetition of this straightforward practice night after night strengthens their bond and reminds them of their positive relationship. Despite everyday living difficulties, their dedication to fostering their love is evident in this modest gesture.

There are many kinds of rituals, from the commonplace to the significant. They may be a weekly ritual of preparing a special dinner, an annual celebration of your anniversary with a weekend getaway, or a morning ritual of having coffee together and discussing the day ahead. The most important thing is that these customs are significant for both spouses and help deepen your bond.

Establishing rituals requires intentionality and a readiness to prioritize your relationship. It's about finding time for one another despite hectic schedules and competing expectations. It's about making room for loving and appreciative sentiments, deep talks, and shared experiences.

Determine the things you both like to do first. Do you enjoy concerts, hiking, cooking, or watching movies? Include these common hobbies in your weekly schedule. Make it a routine to go to a local concert once a month, organize a weekly movie night with a theme, or arrange a monthly Saturday morning trek.

Think about establishing customs around everyday activities. Have a cup of coffee every morning and discuss your plans for the day. After supper, go for a walk together to bond and relieve tension. Before going to bed, curl up on the couch and read a book together. These tiny moments of connection interwoven into your everyday routines create a sense of intimacy and shared experience.

Commemorate important events with heartfelt customs. Establish a unique way to celebrate holidays together, plan a romantic vacation for your anniversary, or make birthdays special. These customs provide enduring memories and signify essential turning points in your relationship.

Additionally, rituals can serve as pillars in trying times. These dependable habits provide security and comfort when disagreements emerge, or life presents unforeseen obstacles. They offer a safe refuge to weather the storms together and serve as a reminder of your relationship's solid foundation.

For instance, following a fight, a couple may make it a habit to stroll together. This gives them a calm environment to relax, digest their feelings, and reconnect. As an alternative, they may establish a monthly ritual of having a special lunch together, which would serve as a space for candid conversation and a reminder of their devotion to one another.

Ritual creation is a creative and individualized process. There needs to be a correct or incorrect method. The most crucial element is that the rituals you establish are significant for both parties and help deepen your relationship.

Here are a few ritual examples to get you thinking:

- "Good Morning" Texts: Send your significant other a heartfelt text message to start each day.

- Weekly Date Nights: Set aside a specific night every week to spend time together without interruptions.

- "Check-In" Talks Every Month: Set aside time every month to talk about your relationship, your objectives, and any difficulties you may be having.

- Annual Weekend Getaways: Arrange a memorable vacation every year to commemorate your anniversary or spend time together.

- Gratitude Rituals: Write down or speak out three things you are thankful for daily.

- Affectionate Touch Rituals: Make it a point to give each other regular hugs, kisses, or cuddles.

- Shared Hobby Rituals: Participate in an activity or pastime you like, such as hiking, cooking, or gaming.

- "Tech-Free" Rituals: Establish specific times or locations when you put technology aside and concentrate on spending quality time together.

These are but a handful of instances to get you thinking. Finding rituals, you and your partner find meaningful is crucial because it builds shared experiences and deep connections that improve and deepen your relationship.

Key Points

- It takes deliberate action and constant work to create a culture of love and respect, not just the lack of disagreement.

- When you show your mates how much you value them vocally and physically, you create a positive and affirming environment in your relationship.

- Maintaining a good relationship requires respecting your partner's boundaries, values, and opinions—even if they diverge from yours.

- A loving and respectful relationship is built on open and honest communication, which includes active listening and a readiness to comprehend your partner's viewpoint.

- Establishing tiny and large rituals of connection improves your relationship and gives you a sense of security and purpose.

Self-Reflection Questions

1. How frequently do you thank your significant other? Do you take note of and appreciate the contributions they make to the relationship?

_____

_____

_____

_____

_____

2. Even when your partner's views and boundaries diverge from your own, how well do you respect them?

_____

_____

_____

_____

3. How well do you express your demands and emotions to your significant other? Do you communicate honestly and clearly?

_____

_____

_____

_____

4. How do you usually react when your significant other communicates their wants or worries? Do you listen to them with compassion and try to comprehend their viewpoint?

_____
_____
_____
_____
_____

5. Do you and your partner engage in any connection rituals? Could you establish new customs to improve your connection and fortify your relationship?

_____
_____
_____
_____
_____

Conclusion

As you finish this book, we hope you have a new appreciation for the role of conflict in your relationship. Conflict, frequently regarded as a warning of doom, a sign that something is wrong, is an unavoidable companion on the path of love. It follows us like a persistent shadow through the ups and downs, joys and tragedies, ordinary moments, and significant milestones that create our shared life.

However, unlike a shadow, which duplicates our actions, conflict provides a unique chance for growth, understanding, and deeper connection. It is a mirror that reflects our unique needs, values, and vulnerabilities. It's a crucible in which love is tried and purified, becoming more substantial and robust.

Throughout this book, we've examined the complex dance of conflict in partnerships. We've reviewed the anatomy of a fight, the science of connection and disconnection, and the distinct conflict cultures we each bring to our collaborations. We've discussed the value of emotional awareness, the art of communication, and the need to provide a safe environment for vulnerability. We've provided:

- Tools and methods for negotiating common conflict scenarios.
- Learning the art of compromise.
- Viewing conflicts as growth opportunities.

The route of love is not a smooth, paved highway; instead, it is a meandering, occasionally rocky road with unexpected twists and turns. Conflict is unavoidable in this terrain, resulting from two people with different perspectives and desires attempting to navigate life's road together.

However, confrontation does not have to be destructive. When approached with intention, respect, and want to understand, it can catalyze greater intimacy, stronger relationships, and a more rewarding partnership.

Remember the main principles we've discussed:

- Acknowledge your emotions. Pay attention to your own and your partner's sentiments.

Emotions transmit essential information about your wants and boundaries.

- Communicate clearly and respectfully: Be honest and direct about your thoughts and feelings while respecting your partner's point of view. Use "I" phrases, avoid blaming, and actively listen.

- Create a safe space for vulnerability: Build trust and respect in your relationship, allowing both partners to share their concerns, doubts, and dreams.

- Seek compromise and understanding: When disagreements arise, approach them to find solutions that work for both of you. Empathize, set boundaries, and celebrate your accomplishments.

- Reframe conflict as an opportunity: See disagreements as opportunities to learn, grow, and strengthen your relationship. Accept the challenges and believe you will emerge from conflict more robust and united.

These ideas, like tools in a well-stocked toolbox, can guide you through love's inevitable ups and downs. They can help you turn conflict from a source of division into an opportunity for growth, intimacy, and a more resilient partnership.

The path of love and conflict is an ongoing experience, a never-ending dance of connection and disconnection, harmony and discord. There will be periods of irritation, hurt, and confusion. There will be times when you feel lost, detached, or unsure about how to proceed.

But, even in these difficult times, remember the importance of connection. Remember the love that links you, the shared dreams that motivate you, and the dedication that underpins your partnership. Reach out to one another, provide support, and seek understanding. Lean on the tools and tactics you've learned, and believe in your capacity to overcome the obstacles together.

Conflict, while unavoidable on the path of love, does not have to define your partnership. With intention, compassion, and a willingness to learn and grow, you may turn arguments into stepping stones, resulting in a love that deepens, strengthens, and thrives amidst life's inevitable storms.

As you end this book, we want to leave you with a message of hope and encouragement. Your relationship, like a plant, requires ongoing care. There will be periods of vigorous growth followed by periods of hibernation. There will be times when weeds attempt to overpower the delicate blooms, and storms of turmoil threaten to uproot the very foundation of your relationship.

However, with patience, love, and a commitment to nourishing your relationship, you can weather these storms and emerge more robust and beautiful on the other side. Accept the trials, cherish the victories, and remember that the journey of love, intricacies, and inconsistencies is the most exciting adventure.

THANK YOU

Dear Readers,

Thank you for choosing to read this book. It has been an honor to share these ideas with you. I hope this book will help you manage the intricacies of love and conflict, lay a stronger foundation for your relationship, and develop a more rewarding and resilient partnership.

If you found this book helpful, please consider leaving a review. Your feedback helps other couples discover this resource and begin their journey of deeper connection and understanding.

Thank you again for accompanying me on this journey through love and strife. I wish you all the best on your ongoing journey of growth and connection.

With warm regards,
Myron Wingen.

Milton Keynes UK
Ingram Content Group UK Ltd.
UKHW021012291124
451807UK00015B/1214